MW00583263

HOW TO USE YOUR 5 SENSES
TO TRIGGER YOUR HAPPY ANYWHERE, ANYTIME.

BY EMILY WYANT

Mention of specific companies, organizations, or authorities in this book does not imply endorsement by the author or the publisher, nor does mention of specific companies, organizations, or authorities imply that they endorse this book, its author, or the publisher.

Internet addresses and telephone numbers given in this book were accurate at the time it went to press.

Happy by Design Jingle
Noah & Annie, noaniemusic@gmail.com
Book formatting & Design
Hicham Hamzi at H-Hich Design, hhichdesign@gmail.com
Book coach
Jill L. Ferguson,
jill@jillferguson.com

© 2021 by Emily Wyant

Printed in the United States.

ISBN - 978-1-7340635-0-9 paperback
ISBN - 978-1-7340635-1-6 e-book
ISBN - 978-1-7340635-2-3 audio book

Author's Note

This book is dedicated to my loving grandmother, Marion Elizabeth Vasquez (August 25, 1929 to February 19, 2018)

She was an extraordinary woman and I can only strive to be as wonderful as she was.

What I remember the most about her was that she never complained about anything. She always had a smile on her face, and if there was negativity in the air, she was quick to change the subject.

During arguments, she would sit still until it was over and move forward with something good to say. She came of age during the Great Depression and World War II and this shaped the person she became. Remember when the men went to war without choice and the women became dedicated nurses? Nationwide in life you were to stand strong together no matter what. This generation came from a life of hard work when things were structured to last, including relationships. Today, we are flooded by the paradox of choice. My grandmother's character was something we can all learn from today. Her level of self-discipline showed through etiquette and proper posture. Posture is something that I notice often, it tells me this person is strong physically and isn't lazy. During that time, it was unacceptable to tell others if you were facing hard times in your life, and even if troubles were brewing, you were to conduct yourself with dignity and put a smile on your face. Her level of self-control came from years of practice in a world of difficulty. Her father died when she was 13, and she was the oldest of six children. Her generation held strong through duty, honor, courage, and family. They shaped a great world for the generation after them. They were considered to be the greatest generation that society ever built.

I recognize her influence on my life. I was her protégé from day one. I remember a story my mom told me about when I was about two years old. I would watch everything my grandma did and I would copy one thing in particular: the "grocery bag fluff." Being the woman that she was, she didn't waste anything. When we got back from the grocery store, she would put everything away and also fold up the plastic grocery bags and place them neatly in the bottom drawer, saving them for reuse in smaller garbage cans around the house. But before she would fold them, she would fluff them in the air much like fluffing clothes so they would lay and fold right. So, you know what I would do every time I saw one of those grocery bags? That's right, I would walk around the house fluffing the grocery bags in the air like Grandma did. Everyone thought it was the cutest thing. I think there may be a video of it somewhere. Staying with Grandma and cooking with grandma was special. When I got a little older, about 6, she bought me an ABC cookbook so I could learn while we cooked. A, for Apple Crisp and C, for Chocolate Chip Cookies were my two favorites.

My grandmother lived by example and designed life of her own happiness. She always had a huge smile to greet her guests and passersby on the street; she had a happy soul. Her resting face was with a smile. She practiced maturity her whole life; she sat up straight with her hands folded like a lady was supposed to. I was always told, "Emmy, sit up straight and don't slouch!" She did this because she wanted me to put my best self forward; I see that now. She was a great bowler; the home office was filled with trophy from years and years of bowling. She loved to bowl and play cards. She had a small purple sack she kept all of her spare change in so she would be ready for the quarter bets. She even taught me to play. The generation gap between us is what made her influence on me easier to absorb. I wished I was able to have her around longer, but everything is as it should be. If I had any more time, I may not have viewed it as beneficial.

My grandmother expected that we finish what we put on our plates and that we waste nothing. A healthy lifestyle included daily exercise, keeping a clean, organized home, and living within your means. I will never forget waking up most mornings to my grandma in the living room working out to Jane Fonda in front of the television.

She had this little wooden square ab-twisting thing she would stand on and twist her abs to Jane in the living room. Between you and me, I think my grandpa made it for her, because it didn't look store bought. He was handy like that. I would often walk by where she kept it and pull it out for a little twisting myself.

After working out, we would have breakfast outside in the backyard. I would spread out the bird-seed, and we would watch the birds eat while we had our breakfast. My grandpa named them peepers. We would make a little peep peep peep sound just like he taught us and they would come over for small pieces of bread. After breakfast, we would clean up and make the beds before our walk. Never leave the house a mess was a rule and always come back home to a tidy home was a great way to live by. Off to our walk around the neighborhood, in the peaceful Menlo Park, Sharon Heights, California. We would walk and admire everyone's gardens and always stop to smell the flowers; red roses were her favorite. She would take me down to the jungle gym to play and then back on our walk. My most memorable part of our walks was holding hands, and every time we'd see a pole or something that would split us up, we would say bread and butter, p.b. and j., cake, and ice cream! We were so cute! Everyone in the neighborhood knew Grandma. She would stop and chat with everyone she knew. Halfway through our walk, we would arrive at the Sharon Pond, the most beautiful park I've ever seen. A huge fountain sits in the middle with a little island in the pond, and tons of ducks and turtles and people walking around. The greenery was so beautiful and the water blue; it was like you were in a dream. If you ever get a chance to see Sharon Pond, I highly recommend it, especially if you have children. I took my grandmother on her last walk to it before she passed, and it was on

Thanksgiving Day in 2018, right after I cooked her last Thanksgiving dinner. She always had every single meal prepared for all holidays and every day in between.

My grandma raised me to never forget my manners at all costs. We were taught to treat others with love and respect, and that if you didn't have anything good to say, not to say anything at all. (I don't always follow this, but I'm working on it, re-parenting myself to become who I want to be.)

In September 2016, my mother informed me that my grandmother would need 24-hour care. She asked if I wanted to move in with my grandmother. I took a day to consider the impact it would have on my life and hers. It is the full circle of life: you take care of your family, especially an angel like my grandmother. I didn't see anything holding me back. My business was doing well. I had no husband or children, and I lived alone. I was no longer wasting my life with drugs and alcohol, thanks in part to my grandmother. I was focused and present.

My grandmother taught me to cook from scratch and to infuse the food with your soul. What better way to give back for all of the wonderful things she did for me? It made logical sense for me to move in and cook for my grandmother. Not only was it the right thing to do, it was an opportunity to share my love and energy with the woman who gave me nothing but her best.

Over the course of the next 14 months, we went go on slow walks and when we needed to went on wheelchair rides throughout the neighborhoods, just like we did when I was a kid. She didn't let one person walk by without greeting them with her charm. We wore wigs on Wednesdays. We smoked candy cigarettes and put on facemasks to keep ourselves beautiful. Our hearts overflowed with so much joy, love, and laughter.

My grandma and I shared a very special bond, I went on to film my first videos for my YouTube channel there at the Sharon Pond. It was months after her passing and I was really nervous because I had never been on camera before. My hair business is something I have been passionate about most of my life. When I decided to do hair, my grandma was the first person I thought about it with. After we decided it was a great idea, I was able to be the one to do her perms and roller-sets at the Cosmetology School where she went to have her hair done once a week. It was time to spread the word on camera about the world of hair by Emily Wyant, CEO of Bond Hair Bar.

I thought, what a wonderful place to have an outdoor video; it was sentimental also.

That morning at 9 a.m. as everyone arrived and began setting my camera crew, my video crew, and video coach: Crystal Lindsay, her husband along with my first model for the day who has been a client and friend of mine for many, many years, Christine. We all couldn't help but to take in the beauty of our surroundings. Everyone was in awe as they had never been there before. Christine had mentioned she wished she had known how breathtaking it was and would have brought her son and husband to see the turtles and ducks. After about 10 minutes of taking it all in, I noticed something that I will never, ever forget. I noticed single red roses floating in the water; they were popping up all over the place. It was about one dozen red roses. I suddenly got chills and knew my grandma was there. Needless to say, everything flowed perfectly that day. I had the energy from my grandma reminding me that I am her little pumpkin.

I live the life of happiness in her honor. She filled her life with all things that made her happy, and in turn, she made those around her happy also.

I learned how to do this from her, and how to design a happy life. That is why I dedicate this book to her and call it *Happy by Design*.

How to Design Your Happy

No one is responsible for your own happiness, but you. Sometimes staying happy all the time can be a challenge. When life kicks us off our asses, we better have a game plan in place. Let's be ready to snap back into action with something fun and keep 'em guessing. Let's give ourselves a real treat and dance our way right over the finish line. You know, show off a little. Let's let all of those naysayers, say, "What's he or she so happy about?" Or, "I'll take some of what she's having!"

We all know it's a challenge to stay happy all the time unless we're meditating all day to melt the stress away. With the working class working, the stay at-home moms/dads leading the home front, and those of us who are juggling both, the load can be heavy. With commutes, cooking schedules, the clean up crew and the continuous organizing, it seems we have no time for ourselves. The more responsibilities we add, the further away from fun we get. The further from fun we are, the closer we are to things brewing. Before you know it, we've hit our boiling points. And we wonder how we got there. Whether you're verbal and your lid flies off and hits everyone in the room or you are one for the silent treatment and you sit there building more pressure, either way, when the shit hits the fan, you wished it hadn't. It is not a good look, is it?

We all process stress differently, but any way you process it, the effects on our nervous systems are poisonous. The most common way today to deal with stress of any form is through self-medication, which is sometimes in the form of instant gratification. Today there are plenty of unhealthy avenues to relieve the pain. I know, as I've been there plenty in my lifetime. I see it now as two wrongs are just wrong. If we keep going the wrong direction over and over, where do we end up?

Divorced, in jail, jobless, homeless, in the nuthouse, living in your own personal hell, or even worse, suicide. Some of the outwardly happiest, funniest people in the world are the most inwardly unhappy and want it to end. It's happening more and more these days.

Wouldn't it be nice to be able to beat the blues back with a personal mind-fuck and come out gleaming on the other side? After all, our mind fucks us all the time, so why can't we take control of it? Let's say goodbye to losing our shit and fuck some fun into our lives, why don't we?

We've forgotten who we are. Remember the good old days, back when we didn't have responsibilities? What did we enjoy then? Martha Beck reminds us that most of the things we enjoyed as children we'd still enjoy today if our egos didn't scream that we can't do those things because we are now adults. Did you like to climb trees or swing on swings? Did you skip down sidewalks singing songs with your friends or find a quiet corner in which to read? I want to see you light up your life. I mean really light it up. Embrace your inner child and your childhood activities and reclaim your delight.

As a child living in a household of divorce, I can thank my lucky stars I had things like roller skating, singing and dancing to Whitney Houston, and giving my Barbie dolls punk rock hair cuts to enjoy my time. Now the things that make me happy are still very similar to the things I enjoyed as a child, but a little more grown up. I love the idea of making a list of all the things we enjoyed as children and see how they apply today. I often hear that we end up doing what we loved doing as children, eventually. It took me 10 years of working in tech to remember how much I loved hair and beauty as a child. And it all started with those Barbie dolls and then moved into being the family hair stylist to my two brothers. Tommy had the Vanilla Ice zings on the sides and Jonny wore a duck tale for years! What was in us then never changed, just our surroundings did. Food for thought.

Some of us aren't prepared with what makes us happy. It is important to know our triggers and become aware of how we deal or not. I used to drink and smoke myself into a fun place during high school. I also took drugs and got into relationships with men who weren't good for me and who weren't concerned with me living my best life. Through the help of my grandmother and by going through a treatment program in my early 20s, I was able to learn to find happiness in other, healthier things. That old saying rings true, we substitute one for the other quite often. Now, with so much instant influence at our finger tips, it's more important than ever that we see what we are actually using as substitute and ask ourselves, is it really good for our health?

How we treat ourselves is how we are able to see the world around us and this begins to shape the person we are and who we can become on so many levels. We can either hold ourselves back or push ourselves forward with the choices we make. I realized when I was in the presence of people who were encouraging me to take drugs, to steal, and to behave badly, I didn't like myself very much. Once I decided to de-friend those influences and found happiness in better ways, I started to trust myself and to like the person I was shaping into. Have you had those mornings when you regret the things you continue to do on a daily basis over and over again and never give yourself the chance to actually wake up happy about your life and the choices you make? It begins to feel like dark clouds over your character as if you are suffocating the person you are supposed to be. For example, you know you need to stop eating junk food because it doesn't make you feel good and you're gaining weight and feeling terrible as the days go on. It all starts with one decision of enough is enough. List out what you want to leave behind and list what you want to add and read it aloud every day. I'm sure the change will come sooner than you think. This will make you very happy and feel stronger than ever. If you can't do it alone, tell a friend or call a hotline; a support system exists for everything. As humans, we want to be of service naturally; it fills our spirits with joy.

How do you appeal to yourself? Whom do you want to become? Do you have someone you look up to, whom you wish you were more like? Don't leave it up to your environment to decide your life and fate. After my grandmother passed away, naturally I was very upset and my friend Bob gave me some very comforting insight on coping with the death of a loved one. He suggested that I take the one thing about her that I admired the most and replace it with something I disliked about myself. This would be my way of keeping her alive within myself. What a touching thing to do.

We all have choices and we make them every day. Our choices pave our paths. Did you know that more than 88 percent of people are absorbing environmental toxicity and don't even know it? Some toxicity we don't have control over, but most of it we do.

What we upload on autopilot sends messages to our brains which in turn operates our bodies. Our brains are our bodies' operating systems, just like a CPU in a computer. Our program works from the outside-in and inside-out sequence. What are things that bring you joy on contact? To design your personal program, think of your five senses as your "control panel", or a major part of your nervous system. Your senses are your control panel to your individual happiness, and like your DNA, no two control panels are exactly the same.

We can learn to program ourselves using only the things that make us happy. Enjoy your design; it's yours for life. Learn what makes you happy and how to control it anywhere, anytime. It is my hope that you focus on your happiness often.

I cannot wait to hear about what makes you happy because that helps make me happier. I am sitting on the edge of my seat and my butterflies are going nuts. This book isn't even published yet, but thinking about your happiness brings me joy.

Let me paint a picture for you. When you are going to an event, whether it be a concert, a conference, or a play, you receive a program of events. What if you were able to make your own program, your personal best day ever, best life ever program? Many of us do what we "need" to do for money to live, but are we living? Ask yourself: What would I do if money was no object? What would I do? Where would I be? Where would I wake up? What would I do first? What would

I fill my day with? It's time to throw everything out the window and start from a blank piece of paper and a clear mind. Take whatever is on your Etch-a-Sketch and shake it up for a clean screen. Sit in a quiet place, in your office, bedroom, or lock yourself in the broom closet. Get your phone out and set a timer for three minutes. Have a blank screen on your computer or a pen and paper ready to roll, and set the timer. Close your eyes and breathe, relax yourself, enjoy the comfortable personal space. Take five minutes or however long you need to relax. Start to imagine your life from this moment forward as a movie and you are the star in your own film. What happens? I did this exercise at the Best Year Ever conference and it changed the game for me. I hope it will help you imagine your true self, a superstar.

In the exercise, you don't have to work and your life is completely yours to live as you wish. I encourage you to think about this no matter what, even if your life is not at this point. This is your own personal exercise and no one will judge the results (and you shouldn't either). The results will be shocking, and I'm quite sure they will make you feel alive and excited to move forward.

When you're thinking, I encourage you to start writing as soon as the timer sounds. Give yourself 10-15 minutes or so to write your perfect day and have fun with it, dang it!

Imagine my Highest FUTURE

Here's my example

Me as a superstar in my best movie

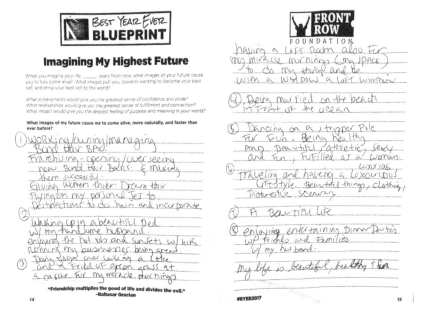

1) Working/owning/managing Bond Hair Bar

-Franchising - opening/overseeing New Bond Hair Bars and making them successful.

-Giving women their dream hair

-Flying on my private jet to different destinations to do hair and incorporate

2) Waking up in a beautiful bed with my handsome husband.

Enjoying the hot tub and sunsets with him.

Running my own business while being great at it.

3) Doing yoga overlooking a Lake and a field of green grass in front of a castle for my miracle mornings

Having a loft room also for my miracle mornings (my private space) also with a window, a loft window.

4) Being married on the beach in front of the ocean

5) dancing on a stripper pole for fun. Being healthy, beautiful, athletic, sexy and fun. Fulfilled as a woman.

6) Traveling and having a luxurious lifestyle. Having beautiful things; clothing and picturesque scenary

7) A beautiful life

8) Enjoying entertaining dinner parties with friends and family with my husband

My life is beautiful, healthy and fun.

Ask yourself another great question, "If money were no object... what would I do or buy?"

Here's an example of my "if money were no object" writing exercise. But don't laugh, I do dream big and that's what it's all about. You are a star and you will make your dreams come true after you're aware of what those dreams are.

If Money was No Object, by Emily Wyant.

I would wake up in Hawaii a lot of the time. I would be a neighbor with my family. My mom, brothers, sister-in-law, and my dad and his girlfriend would be my closest neighbors. We would all meet for coffee. I, of course, would wake early to meditate, and then jump on my morning call since having a daily accountability call that helped get me where I am today. Then I would work on my writing, reading, saying my affirmations in the mirror to keep setting the tone. I would grab my morning beverage and walk out to the beach to do my exercise, energizing myself as the sun rises with my local friends.

I would go back to the house and get myself ready for the day. Next, I would make a large family breakfast like I loved to do as a kid, when I thought I was the best chef in all the land. I would brew Kona coffee and slice melon and papaya with a little lime twist. For the main course, some banana macadamia flapjacks are in order. Extra protein, fiber, and wheat germ to keep us healthy. Here comes my dad and Debbie! We're shooting the shit and admiring the beautiful morning. My dad and I are sipping some coffee out on the terrace overlooking the beach. Here comes the rest of the clan. We all sit and enjoy some food together and have family time before we start our day. We clean up and part ways. What a great way to start the day.

I head downtown to Waikiki for an install for a few celebrity weddings. I get to prepare three brides for their beach weddings tomorrow by giving them the hair of their dreams. Here it is now 2 p.m., the perfect time for a seafood salad on the beach while I soak up some sunshine. Swimming leads to surfing rounded up by a little floating. What a fabulous day. It's time for a massage and then a nap on the beach. Wow, that was delightful. I feel so rejuvenated. I jump on the computer and write a little for my book. This is the life of a beach babe. It's great! Time to go buy some fresh tuna for poke taco salads tonight. I'm definitely going walk by the local bakery on my way home and pick up a Haupia Pie (my mom's favorite).

What a beautiful day, rolling into a fabulous night. After dinner, we head down to the nightly movie on the beach; it's '80s flashbacks tonight. I can't wait to see what it is.

That is what my day would look like if money didn't matter. The important thing about this exercise is to make sure the day is made for you. Do something for YOU. And fall in love with treating yourself selfishly, today and every day. It is your life and the happier you are, the more your subconscious prepares and provides for you. When you are doing what your nervous system reads as complete happiness, through all of five of your senses, your cup is full. I want to see full cups around the world.

Fill them to the brim. Overflow them in fact. Life is yours. This is your body, your mind, and your senses to program and design yourself happy every day. This book couldn't have come at a better time since we have technology making things easier for us to communicate and become influenced. Now is a great time and opportunity to choose how we want to be influenced and how to make better choices to allow ourselves to be happier. We don't want to run on autopilot, wandering around allowing the world to program us. We have a choice. Let us choose our happiness and program our own ourselves. Let's walk on sunshine every day.

But how will we identify what is the best and most fun for us? We all know things we enjoy, but it is my thought that it's time to put these things together. Let's create a list of positive activities to reinforce what gives us zest for life. All we need is our designed happy list to use. Not your mom's list, not your dad's, not your husband's or your wife's, not your teachers', not your mentors', not your kids'. Your list. It is your happy to design and use for yourself, and as I said, no two are exactly the same.

In this book, you will learn how to touch each sense with what sparks you happy, to fill your whole being with what might make you jump for joy anywhere, any time. The perfect part of this plan is once you learn more of what you enjoy, you will be able to access your value. Let us laugh more, feel more, see more, taste more, and hear more for ourselves. With your senses held to a higher level, you are on your way to freedom, freedom from your environment. Are you ready for the foolproof plan?

It's time to set ourselves up for success and fill our cup with happy juice and drink it all the time. Who knows, it might work so well, nothing will be able to faze us. That would be quite the valuable trick, wouldn't it? VICTORY!

When creating new habits, our mind can play tricks on us and changes can become challenging. In order for our positive change to be sustainable, it must be fun. So, let's relax and have some fun.

How many times have you known people to try new diet plans or a new way of life, but they don't end up sticking to it? When that happens, many people would say, that we didn't want it badly enough. But the truth is, we do want it badly enough because we set out to do it in the first place. Our brains already went through the pros and cons phase and proved that it's what's best for our lives.

What happens when we set out to make changes to become happier, but we are unsuccessful? I believe it's because we didn't much fun during the process. Having fun during the process of change helps give change enough pizzazz to keep us interested. Fun will help us flow into a pattern that is better than ever before. After all, the reason we try to make changes is so our lives will become easier and healthier. I am a huge advocate for letting situations and processes flow. When things flow for you, the flow will be personal and individual to you and no one else. After all, DNA has specific characteristics and no two strands are alike. That's why no one else could tell you what is going to make you happy, but you. It's like your very own software, and this is your user experience to enjoy. I am excited to introduce what I find to be the gateway of happiness by your own design. The cool part about this method is it's free, and it's owned by you and ready for use. Once we get a simple list started, you can trigger yourself happy anywhere, anytime, and I hope all the time. To make this even more magnificent, what makes you happy will continue to evolve. Over time as you become a better person, your environment will change as well. Your decor, your clothing, your music, your career, and the people you share your time will be helped by your design.

When you starting treating yourself like you are a gift, the universe will, too. Gifts from you and gifts from the world around you is how it should be. Let us start to give gratitude to what we love. Give what you love the awareness it deserves, and we will always receive more.

Have you ever had a bad relationship that ruined your life, or a change of plans that pissed you off? Or maybe you've had a bad hair day or your food order arrived and it was incorrect and inedible. The weather has been known to throw me a bit off-kilter at times, but that is fixable. Hot tubs, fireplaces, and 12 minutes in a tanning bed are some of my fixes for inclement weather. Vitamin D lamps even exist now, and I have one and sit under it while reading and writing. These things are solutions for people who struggle with a little seasonal depression. Life is worth living the way you want. If you love the cold weather, live where winters happen. If you love the heat, move where it is toasty most of the year.

We let these little setbacks affect our thinking and take us to places of negativity. The annoyances boomerang back and forth in our heads and out of our mouths and fill our cells with unhappiness. Negativity ricochets through our bodies like cancer. When unhappiness is present, our abilities to attract what we deserve and want loses power. Our internal source energy is our personal power and holds gifts of our subconscious. That is what our brain's extra space is meant for, and it is only by design that it can function as it was built. We have the ability to magnetize everything we want.

It is only activated when there is a full positive flow through each of our cells as a collective source of power. The ability to magnetize is no joke, and in fact and it happens all the time. Look at Oprah, Steve Jobs, Einstein, etc.

The truth is, happiness has always been a solid part of me. Happiness has always been the core way of the world. Sometimes true happiness lies deep beneath the surface for people. In me, it is often more deep-down than I would like to admit. I would love to help uncover the happiness gift in each one of us so we may use it to shine. May a positive flow guide us in our lives. Luckily for me, I was born of two pretty happy people who made happy children. I was born to be a cheerleader and I'm great at it. Don't get me wrong; people, places, and things do get me down, and when I'm down it doesn't feel good. So, let us fill our cups together and shine brightly for our lives and be who we were born to be.

My family used to think I had ADD or ADHD. I had so much energy I needed to run track for three hours a day to use a quarter of my core energy. So many children are placed on medications in lieu of a healthy diet, one free of processed foods, plenty of water, a lot of exercises and a good mindful skill set.

Now that I have rid my body of all mind-altering substances, I am normal and happy. I drink plenty of water, I have a healthy workout regimen, I follow a plant-based diet, and now my brain is clear. With meditation 25 minutes twice per day for inner peace and calm, I'm sitting on top of the world with a genius tool set. I am now able to use my drive (the mania everyone thought I had) and pour it into achieving goals, like writing books, focusing on the hair business that I love, and creating a better life for myself. I focus on preparing healthy food for myself and staying on regular sleep schedules. Sleep patterns are important to keep in sync with the earth. We are one with the earth.

I am a believer in a baseline healthy lifestyle to see where you stand before using medications. This is an approach people don't have time for these days. I do know that time is our most valuable asset because we can't get it back.

I'm a part of a Morning Hero Mastermind Accountability group that meets Monday through Friday at 5 a.m. on the Internet. Our team leader, Jarvis Leverson, has us do one awareness exercise every day, along with our three goals for the day. I connect with the awareness exercises on a deep level. I spend hours on awareness because they speak to me. They are allowing me to blossom, and I see the progress every day. Hal Elrod says, rarely does your success supersede your level of personal development. We attract our success by the person we become. I didn't take notes on this quote until the second time reading his book. *The Miracle Morning* was the only book I have ever read twice. *The Miracle Morning* has completely changed me life. I had to reread the book a few times to hear important tidbits like this. The mindful assignment on this particular day asked us to think for one minute on why were you born? Everyone has a purpose, a special talent that comes to us, and something that is the core of who we are. My answer after only a few seconds of thought was to make people happy. I have always been excited, adventurous, and the life of the party. I was the one to get detention for being disruptive during class, talking when I wasn't supposed to, passing notes, giggling; you know, I was being a happy kid.

I am happy inside most of the time, but when things get me down, I have trained myself to have faith for the sake of my sanity. I try to see the lesson and the gift in what's happening right here and right now. This wasn't always a natural path for me. This is who I've become over the last several years.

In order for me to design the happy place I first had to think about what are the things that make me happy. So many people don't know what makes them happy, but that's why we're here. I have a friend who has spent his whole entire life doing for others. Today, he struggles with headaches that have been troubling him since his early 20s. He is in his early 60s and still doesn't have time for himself. Or should I say he doesn't "make" the time for himself? I know this behavior to be codependency. Taking a moment to think about it from the outside leads me to wonder: What would he do and what would he feel if he gave himself some him time for himself? The amount of inner self that has been ignored for so long has led him to become okay with not making time for himself. The level of inner depression that has been buried for so many years is better off left behind, he thinks. What about his life brought him to this place? I think he feels selfish and guilty when he does something for himself, and that's why it's a rarity.

Thoughts are the beginning of our breakthroughs. Let us uncover what our environment has done to us and begin to re-create ourselves. To be free of guilt is your freedom. The person you become is yours to choose. True self-happiness is what you decide. Sure, it's lovely to do things for others; it makes us feel good and others feel good. But we can't over-give just as we shouldn't be stingy with giving. To have a balance important. I love being of service to those who will do something with it. Though to be stuck doing nothing for yourself is no way of adding value to yourself, your life, and the ones you love. Be selfish and practice self-care daily. If this rings true for you, please make time for yourself. You can live longer and continue being the caretaker you are more effectively if you take care of yourself first. It all starts with you; this is your universe. Let's be happy and efficient so those around you will notice and absorb the difference. Leading by example and creating awareness are the only ah-ha moments that counts. It's not you telling someone to do something, it's you actually living it that counts. Three times per week is a good balance to spend time on a hobby. To read, to write, to practice discovering what makes you happy, use your personal time and enjoy it.

It is okay if you don't know at the moment what makes you happy. That is why we're going to do this together. Together we will make a list and you will know how you can trigger you to be happy. It will be your private road map to your best self! Give yourself the chance to reflect on who you are and what allows you to be your most admirable self. If you do not know what that is, ask yourself, "Who do you admire and why?" Why not fill yourself with some of those traits, too? Whose personality do you love and why? The discovery process is fun because we're not applying it to ourselves, yet, so it's not that scary.

It's like making a vision board. If you're unfamiliar with vision boards they are pictures and cut out words of the things we want to attract. Same thing here, what does your best self or your best life look like?

The best most valuable part of you is your ability to adapt. We can train ourselves to do most anything. We can train for marathons if we want to. Practice makes perfect. We can practice using someone else's personality traits on ourselves. It's like acting. Shakespeare called "all the world a stage" and we are living in the theatre whether we realize it or not. Using someone else's admirable traits brings you one-step closer towards a better you. Being aware of who we are first and how we come across to others helps our design. The person you would like to be is in your reach and it's easy to attract. But be sure you're doing this not because I or someone else wants you to be a certain way. Adopt the traits that you want, be the way you want to be, and be this way anytime, anywhere, no matter what. No matter what life brings, including twists and turns that aren't comfortable, you can effortlessly turn to something positive. Two things that kill us as humans are stress and inflammation. We will get rid of stress with tips in this book. Not only do the strong survive, but the happy get busy living.

After quite a bit of thought about a real true, deeply happy, I realized this is something that comes from within. If we stimulate all of our senses to make grasping our happy worth doing, we would do it EVERY DAY. If our body thanks us, it shows for all to see, and that's what we want: to create our master SMILE that shows and glows through all of our senses. Our five senses are hearing, sight, touch, smell, and taste. What better way than to design a foolproof route to find this prize-winning smile, our best happy!

Jay Danzie said, "Your smile is your logo, your personality is your business card, how you leave others after an experience with you becomes your trademark." This reminds me of how important our impacts are on those around us. And it all starts with our logo, our smiles. Wouldn't that be cool if our logos were our individual smiles? Maybe we should start a trend. Like wearing a nametag every day if you want to make new friends and open the door to people around you. Just the other night I was at the new rooftop lounge in San Francisco at the Virgin hotel. There was a convention that day for eye doctors, and many people at the lounge were still wearing their nametags. I struck up conversations with those people because I felt like I was invited to. To be able to say hello to someone by name is way cool. Let's start our design by wearing a name tag every day if you want someone to say hello to you. Why not invite the life around you to engage if you want?

Our smiles are one of those small tokens we can give away and make a difference every day with every person we meet. Being happy is one of those things that is free to us, and it's a gift to those around us. Show you are happy today so you can continue spreading it on to others. And when you get a smile back, you can put that in your pocket and have it for the rest of your life.

I like to think of my happy design as my personal user manual and a straight shot to everything I want in my life: the places I want to go, the people I want to meet, and the fun time I'm out to have.

My belief is that our universe is our subconscious and it is here to listen and provide, good or bad. I know from personal experience that when I do something my internal sensors knows is wrong then karma comes ready with my fair shake. Miracles are what I named my good angel and karma is my bad angel. Whichever I chose to give power to is exactly who's driving me home, and I'd like to make it home in one piece, thank you.

After becoming more interested in mediation, I was drawn to Transcendental Meditation as a practice. I've began to research TM, everything about it thoroughly. I began to practice regularly, and I noticed my brain begin to work, running at a level 10. Interesting things began to happen that would surprise me and make me take mental note of "did that really just happen?" Things that were and are happening in my favor like parking spaces right in front of wherever going was noticeably different. Time off to take vacations at just the right time and offers of help exactly when I need it are just a few examples. Some might call these things chance or coincidence, but I call them the universe reminding me I am right where I am supposed to be. I am being handed the opportunity to flow with ease. It seems like I am in the right place at the right time. I like to think of it as being "in the zone". Meditation is one of the most important aspects of being in the zone. It has the ability to clear the noise and remove the viruses we unknowingly upload throughout our day and our life. Let's clear the noise that blocks our universe from connecting to our subconscious. I don't know about you, but I would rather miracles drive me around while I wave like the president at the parade.

But first, we need to clear out all of the undesirable crap that our life has done to us and make space for our new design. Since our experiences shape who we are and experiences dictate what we are afraid of, we need to give ourselves opportunity to control our lives. The feeling I get when I clean my room, my car, and my workspace allows me to be more aware of the toxins in my life. When I see clean and organized, I think clean and organized. I am then able to pinpoint what ails me. If I clean my physical space and then clear my mental space, I'm in a good place. That result I get when I clear fog from my brain with meditation is like taking a wire brush and cleaning the corrosion from my receptors. We need our connectors to conduct at their full capacity. It is like we're all driving sports cars that are meant to go fast and corner like we're on rails. But most of us are not taking it over 30 MPH because our connectors are corroded with rust. We are rusting our connectors because of bad things that have happened that we weren't able to process. Instead we throw in alcohol, street drugs, and prescription pharmaceuticals, junk food, and all kinds of other things we do to numb the pain and forget about what ails us. This is the main reason we have rusty connectors. Every second we aren't skipping down the street with joy, our connectors are getting rusty and we misfire. The longer we stay unhappy or unhealthy our body thinks this is "the norm" and strives to stay that way. We need to connect fully to our presences and enhance naturally. Life is too good to live with rusty connections. Let's let the good times roll and build on that.

Einstein was one of our well-known geniuses. Let's learn from what Einstein did and keep building. Let's use our vehicles for what they were meant to, enjoy our paths and pave them with perfection.

Your Control Panel

Become familiar with your body control panel, your five senses. Our five senses are our bodies' awareness guides of what you like and don't like. Your program to design a life of your own.

Your personal programming is your design. Identifying what makes you happy will be the start of your program. In this book we will go over all sorts of ideas to help build your personal program. With your program, you will be able to connect your subconscious to the universe and do most anything effortlessly.

You will learn how to navigate the magic carpet of life. It is up to do to decide where you go.

Happiness is a state of mind. The process of your five senses working in synergy ultimately dictates your level of happiness. Your sensory system is the heart of your happiness and it can be used to navigate to a healthier happier life; you can learn what brings your five senses joy, and then sync them is your happy place.

Sometimes we feel joy from only one, two, or three of our senses and the other two might not be happy at the moment. If we could explore one sense at a time and really separate the feelings we get, we see what makes our core happy. Isn't that what we want is to be happy to our core? To figure out what our drivers are is our game plan to freedom. Familiarizing ourselves with our control panels gives us the coordinates for our destinations. Direction identifies our primary destination. Systems are meant to be explored and developed for growth. Together we will hit the road on the adventure of a lifetime. So, buckle your seatbelt, I'm hitting the gas and we're going for maximum speed.

Learning what brings you Joy

One of the most well-known teachers for teaching the art of "what brings you joy" is Marie Kondo. If you take sufficient time to explore your own sense of joy, the speed with which you make decisions will accelerate rapidly. My thought is that you get to know yourself better through your senses to become familiar with your "feeling of joy" so you can continually move towards it and not away from it. The key here is to be happy and continue doing things that make us happy. So, we need to "feel" what that feels like.

Marie Kondo says, "Cherish the things you love. Cherish yourself." Find what you truly cherish in life. Cherish who you are and what brings you the most joy and fulfillment. Don't let stuff, or worries, get in the way or distract you from the life you want.

I am usually one to read self-help books because I want to understand more about the world that surrounds me and how to navigate through this world successfully and with joy. I say successfully because I feel that in today's world, we have a pretty good chance of getting caught in whatever distraction might be pulling us away from ourselves. The distractions through modern technology are meant to bring us closer to someone else's life and someone else's feelings, while further from our own. In no time, we will be a "follower" of someone else's life and forget our own. Is that what we really want to do, to become further from our own happiness and follow someone else's? I think we need to say our own name 15 times per day with an affirmation attached. Otherwise, we soon begin to become brainwashed into seeing, thinking, and viewing the world through someone else's body. This isn't good for our self-esteem. The importance of building a bond within ourselves couldn't be more necessary. I've always wondered why people would read fiction, but I understand now reading fiction can be a way to escape. Dreaming big is great after all; dreams become a reality. It wasn't until recently that I've learned more about the world, and I have taken time to dissect what makes me happy and why. I got rid of my television, shut down Facebook, and began to take interest in myself. Now I have the opportunity to share with you a simple outlet for you to access every single day of your life. I believe that the vast majority of us were once happy or are normally happy. In this day and age, we have moved further from nature and calm, and we seek solace in an assortment of manmade entertainment, which can bring us even further from ourselves and closer to addiction of all sorts. People want an escape, and *Happy By Design* is creating your personal entrance and awareness into what makes you happy.

* Let's take this time to your special Happy By Design Personal Notebook at happybydesignbook.com. Here you can take notes about yourself that pop into your head as we go through our five

senses. Anything you can learn about yourself through this book will bring you many steps above the rest. When something pops into your head, write it here in your notebook where you won't forget it so you can remember and use them always to keep your spirit happy always!

You can program your brain with either viruses every day (garbage in, garbage out) or you can keep everything organized and fill yourself with happy thoughts, happy music, happy feelings, and happy people in your life who are giving you good vibes, a life that is bringing you joy. Create your space and make this world your place of value to serve you. Your environment will help your personal growth, set it up just the way you like it. In your bedroom, your office, your vehicle, your bed, your closets, and your kitchen. These are your surroundings; the things you come in contact with are important to furnish and organize with conscious decisions regarding what makes you happy.

Sense of Taste

We should also make conscious decisions about what tastes make us happy. Not only does food provide nourishment for our body, but it provides sustenance for the soul. Eating and tasting are considered pleasurable experiences.

Taste (and smell) sensations are important because they prepare our bodies for digesting our food. When we taste and smell our food, it triggers our salivary glands and prepares our digestive system.

If we couldn't smell or taste, our stomachs wouldn't be ready for food and we would have trouble digesting our meal thus making fuel and nutrient distribution difficult for our bodies.

The very first time I can remember tasting something that brought my taste buds to life was a warm pink sugar called cotton candy. I loved candy so much that my mom used to tell me I was allergic to it so that I would stop eating it. She was concerned because it wasn't good for me, and because it would make my brothers and me so hyper, we would run around completely uncontrollable. My poor mother. We, like most children, were hypnotized by candy. I will never forget the times we went into the department stores as children. We had the time of our lives on outings like this. Our energy at a level seven the second our little toes touched the floor in the morning. We hit the ground running--and sugar only made it worse! We were nightmares for my mom. I'm sure we were the reasons they invented shock collars and child leashes.

And don't even think of taking us into the stores, because you were asking for trouble. To us, going out to the department store or any store for that matter was like taking caged wild animals into the great outdoors. And then you add sugar? Look out Mervyns in Redwood City, here comes some fun! On one particular occasion, my brothers and I snuck some candy in the car before we went out. I'm surprised our parents even allowed sugar in the house, given the effect it had on us. My brother Jonny loved licorice and he would always have a stash on stand-by. If you could imagine three kids ages 9, 7, and 5 sugaring up in the backseat of the 1982 280ZX getting geared up and raring to go!

The excitement anticipating what was about to happen was probably the same thing that goes through an inmate's mind after mastering a prison break for month and then finally having your heyday. This was us on a daily basis, the same thing just kids on candy was the only difference. We arrived and parked. We were mentally synchronized and showing no signs of excitement as we

33

walked as slow as possible holding hands with Mom through the parking lot. Angels on the outside but straight up devil's workshop on the inside. Oh, we had our game faces on all right. As soon as we hit the front door of Mervyns, it was like a gun went off at the races. We dropped hands and shot across the room as fast as we could, jumping from clothing rack to clothing rack like absolute monkeys. You know those old clothing rounders that you could hide in? They don't make them like that anymore. We were popping in and out of those racks like nothing you have ever seen before. We were like we were out of our minds, but we were having fun! It was an adventure. Howling like wolves, taking on the animation of Ninja Turtles like we were running through the streets, fighting bad guys. Again, my mom, poor mom, but we didn't care. We were too juiced up and in our own world. You know how men block out women when they are nagging, this was same thing but with Mom. We were sure not to get caught because then the whole rest of the shopping experience would be like going to Great America and not going on the rides. Boring! We would play tag, hide and go seek, crawl on the floors like the creatures in the night. We would leave no stone unturned in that store. This was our time, our time to be free! This was our own personal amusement park. Remember those days?

Before you knew it, we were in trouble by someone who worked there. One of us would have knocked something down or broken some merchandise. Oh, back when there were rules.

So, you see, candy was fun and it still is; it just turns us into older more mature monkeys now!

I'm sure you have some childhood memories. Why not take a moment and call someone from your childhood to reminisce the good old days? Makes you wonder what might be missing today. Is it candy?

Grandmother used to cook us kids all kinds of treats, and we would look forward to them because they brought us so much joy. From our mouths to our tummies, the sugars would chemically release. Not too long ago, I learned through research that serotonin, one of the brain's neurotransmitter, is a feel-good chemical, and it is estimated that 90 percent of the body's serotonin is made in the digestive tract, hence the reason grandma's cookies were always at the top of my happy list.

After all, who hasn't gotten angry or upset and wanted nothing other than a super-sized sundae drizzled with chocolate sauce to calm down? We use food to affect our moods all the time without even thinking about what we are doing. But more importantly, our daily nutritional intake can have huge impacts on how we feel, and most of that is due to a little chemical called serotonin.

Can you train your brain to make you happier? Try simple tips for working with natural chemical building blocks to boost the feel-good factor, whether you want to feel more secure, crave respect, or need a quick happy high.

the Gift of Taste / The Gift of No Taste?

I couldn't imagine if I wasn't able to taste a good chocolate chip cookie or my morning coffee. We should remember to appreciate the little things like our natural body sensors and functions; after all, that's what we're here for and that's what we've been given to enjoy.

I love coffee and I get my daily jolt of caffeine this way, as caffeine is one of my main ways to increase my body's use of dopamine. While caffeine doesn't increase your production of dopamine, it likely works by making more receptors available to use the dopamine your body produces. I prefer Kona coffee to the taste of teas, a glass of almond milk with some protein powder, a green juice, or just plain water with lemon in the morning. I always start my morning with a lot of water with a pinch of sea salt and some flax seeds that have soaked in my water overnight; it's a great source of fiber and good for a healthy digestive track, too. Taste water, my friends, and taste it all day because it is the source of life, and given to us by our planet. If you feel unhappy, please make an effort to add water to your healthy *Happy by Design* plan, as I know it will help. I promise.

Surely everyone has that special beverage or food that really brings a sense of enjoyment to your days. Lately, I've been so busy I've found myself rushing my morning coffee, rushing my lunch, and then I get into a routine of eating fast and that turns into a lifestyle. When out with friends, I need to be sure I pace myself and not gobble my food like I've been accustomed to lately. This whole fast-paced lifestyle of the Silicon Valley has got to slow down. It's like, who has time to chew?

When we aren't mindful with our food, our taste buds aren't appreciated nor is the food we are tasting. Our taste buds are important sensory items in tasting our food and sending messages to our brain to trigger a chemical release of yum, happy, gross or hot or cold. At any rate, food can make us happy through raising our serotonin levels. For example, Brazil nuts are high in selenium and also include the amino acid tyrosine that both help to boost dopamine and serotonin levels that make us feel happy through our stomachs. That's how a lot of us can become overweight, too much feel-good and not enough health and exercise. Our stomach is the biggest producer of feel-good chemicals. Soup is one of my favorite things to cook, because I love warm foods over cold foods (like salads) always unless it's hot out; then ice cream is key for my food-induced happiness. Comfort foods tend to make me more relaxed and also are heavy enough to give a "sleepy feeling" or a "carb crash". According to WebMD, if you have trouble sleeping you should eat a carb-enriched meal before bedtime to get you nice and sleepy. Having a belly stuffed with comforting food can feel like a warm hug from the inside. As food intake increases, the stomach becomes full, the blood glucose levels change, and the hormone ghrelin, which stimulates appetite, calms down. If you try to get into bed early, have dinner closer to bedtime, it's sure to get you nice and sleepy.

This relatively new research focuses on leptin and ghrelin, two metabolic hormones that scientists discovered only during the last decade. When we eat, leptin signals that the body is satisfied, while ghrelin stimulates hunger. Researchers speculate that if we have enough leptin to suppress the secretion of ghrelin, we'll sleep through the night without awakening to eat. Take note if you're having troubles sleeping or you wake up and can't go back to sleep. I know a lot of people who have this problem so I wanted to touch on the subject. The key to a happy life is getting enough sleep. Leptin is from the Greek work leptos which means thin. Many health problems occur from carrying extra pounds. Being happy is a reflect of being healthy so let's learn what tastes make us healthy and happy. Leptin is an important hormone that regulates appetite and a healthy body weight. Leptin resistance is very common in obese or overweight people and it is usually manifested by increased leptin levels in the blood.

Foods that stimulate leptin sensitivity are: grapefruit, hot peppers, lean proteins, green tea, low fat yogurt, broccoli, almonds, eggs, fruits, vegetables, olive oil, turmeric, apples, purple sweet potatoes, spirulina algae, and sesame seeds. You can also boost your metabolism by eating unprocessed oatmeal.

Scientists studying that good feeling after eating call it "ingestion analgesia," literally pain relief from eating. Dr. Gene-Jack Wang, M.D., the chair of the medical department at the U.S. Department of Energy's Brookhaven National Laboratory, in Upton, New York, says that the ingredients in purified modern food cause people to "eat unconsciously and unnecessarily," and will also prompt an animal to "eat like a drug abuser [uses drugs]." So, it's really important that we are paying attention to what our whole foods are providing for our bodies.

Since the ghrelin makes us hungrier, we should watch our intake of the foods that produce it such as: sweet breads, crackers, cheese, juice, low fat anything, foods labeled "healthy", processed sugar, artificial sweeteners (they leave your body in the same form they enter), fast food, store-bought soups, and alcohol.

If you don't have time to make something from scratch, then just have a small serving of whatever you're craving. Here's what I do, if I'm craving chocolate ice cream, I have a piece of dark chocolate instead. It's still a happy treat until I can get into the habit of having natural fruits around which are better for my body and provide brain power, and most importantly, my body knows how to process them, which is key. All of these mass-produced factory foods were designed to kill off the masses. So, let's eat less of the those and train ourselves to eat more of the things that will keep us healthy and happy through our sense of taste.

Warm things like my favorite whole made soups and hot teas make me feel nice and settled, sort of mindful also. I know warm things make me happy and can absolutely give me a sense of enjoyment better than eating something unhealthy.

Water is at the top my most valuable list of things I put into my body and silly it has no taste, that's why I think most people don't drink enough of it. If you add your favorite fruit or herb to your water it can turn to be the best gift you can give to your taste buds and it will curb your cravings and keep you healthy forever.

I like lemon in water but, lately I've been using apple slices because I know this is what my body needs to process my foods, to flush my body of toxins from the air I breath and the foods I eat. Water is the fountain of youth. In your list of happy, add healthy into each of your senses. We have a list of what we "need" before our "wants". When I began learning about water, it was when I knew it was time to redesign my life and what better structure than to start with my five senses.

Having ample hydration is really important in staying happy. According to one my favorite books *Your Body's Many Cries for Water* by F. Batmanghelid, your body having ample hydration is key in being happy. A pinch of sea salt and water will keep your cells hydrated so you don't get sluggish and you have plenty of natural energy. Through this book, I learned that over 75% of our society is chronically dehydrated.

Dr. Batmanghelid speaks of the brain needing the most hydration because it's in charge of sending messages to the organs for proper body operation. A pinch of sea salt in every glass of water will keep your brain membranes hydrated so it doesn't pull water from your other organs when your hydration gets too low. When the body doesn't have enough water in the brain, we get low on energy and think we're depressed, but we're really dehydrated. As Dr. Batmanghelid writes in his book:

—fear, anxiety, insecurity, persistent emotional and matrimonial problems—and the establishment of depression are the results of water deficiency to the point that the water requirement of brain tissue is affected. The brain uses electrical energy that is generated by the water drive of the energy-generating pumps. With dehydration, the level of energy generation in the brain is decreased. Many functions of the brain that depend on this type of energy become inefficient. We recognize this inadequacy of function and call it depression. This "depressive state" caused by dehydration can lead to chronic fatigue syndrome. This condition is a label put on a series of advanced physiological problems that are seen to be associated with stress.

I quote him all the time in hopes it will help people and it is a great tip that worked for me, when I quit drinking. I wanted to add the opposite of dehydration and hydrate so it's important to positively reinforce what we're trying to achieve by learning about it while we're doing it. So, I read this book and started drinking my water just like he said and I lost eight pounds in three weeks with just adding the correct amount of water to my diet. I love this man, his book, and all of his knowledge as it is helping raise awareness through logical medical information about how our bodies works. Complete genius!

And as I said before that I love coffee, I need to acknowledge that caffeine isn't the greatest so be sure to compensate with more water. (Two cups of water for every cup of coffee.)

The book is a great read that I highly suggest perusing. I've read it three times and bought it three times and I end up giving it to people I meet that need it for some reason, like my friend Monica has had eczema her whole life. Drinking sea salt and water has changed that for her because the beverage keeps the body and its cells hydrated enough to where the organs have the correct amount of water and the skin is fully hydrated, also.

So, sea salted soups because they are filled with water are very good for us. That's why it's been said for years when you're sick eat chicken soup because of the salt content. The idea when we are under the weather is that we need to "flush" what is ailing us out. Keeping the body hydrated and flushing is key to relieve and prevent sickness. We all ultimately want to be happy, and sometimes with our busy lifestyles, we forget the big things that keep us healthy and happy like water or things made with lots of water, like soup. And water keeping us healthy makes complete sense since we are 80 percent water anyway. We need half our body's weight in ounces per day with a pinch of sea salt to keep our bodies functioning at a baseline normal. When I started drinking the correct amount of water, my weight dropped eight pounds, just from giving my body what it needed to live. It took three weeks from my body to get out of a chronic state of dehydration. That was the day my new life took center stage.

When I get stressed and overworked, I'm usually under nourished, and under rested. Fortunately, there are plenty of foods with proven mood-boosting benefits that can help you get happier and healthier with every bite. In times like these, vitamin B-12 is your best friend. Many foods naturally have B-12 so you don't have to take supplements. I love conversing with nutritionists and vitamin suppliers about the need to take supplements. Okay, some don't have great diets, but our bodies absorb the nutrients from the food we eat better than it does many supplements. If our Creator or planet wanted us to take supplements, the gods would have hung them from the trees. And oh, that's right, they did; they're called fruits. Here's how I look at it: plants grow through a photosynthesis process. They get nutrients from the soil, through water, and from sunlight, like we do. Many foods are alkalizing foods; they alkalize our systems like we're supposed to be taking in an alkaline-based diet. Let's go back to the how we're 80 percent liquid, sort of making us a fish tank. Unless a tank of water stays at its natural healthy pH balance, algae will grow and the water will have bacteria and things will start growing in the off-balanced water; it won't be clear anymore. Our bodies are a lot like this; if our pH is off, then disease and cancers start to grow. Another healthy tip, is that we need to eat deep dark green leafy veggies like arugula, Swiss chard, kale, and broccoli or basically anything that tastes bitter and like grass because they are high in chlorophyll and produce oxygen in our blood and body. Cancers cannot grow in an oxygenated area. Love your body with healthy foods, and it will love you back by making you happy.

So, let's taste things that bring health to our bodies and our minds so we can live happily through all of our senses. In a nutshell, we eat our medicine so let's learn about how eating and tasting can keep us mentally and physically healthy and happy. The following are some examples:

Fishes rich in vitamin B-12 are salmon, mackerel, sardine, herring and tuna. 100 grams of salmon provide over 300% of the daily-recommended amount of this essential nutrient. Fish was put on this earth for us to eat and we should eat it regularly to get our source of vitamin B-12 and to get you out of an "angry mood."

Beets contain betaine, which supports serotonin production in the brain, elevating your mood along the way.

Seaweed—yes, like in sushi or on the side as a salad—is packed with depression-fighting iodine, which isn't always so easy to find in food. Iodine is critical for your thyroid to function properly, and the thyroid influences your energy, weight, and even your brain functions a whole lot happier.

Chamomile tea not only brings on better sleep but improves your cognitive functioning during the day, too.

Blueberries just so happen to be a great source of resveratrol, an antioxidant with dark pigment that aids in relief from depression.

Eggs are loaded with mood-stimulating omega-3 fatty acids, zinc, B vitamins, and iodine. Eggs are packed with protein; they'll also keep you feeling full and satisfied for a long time.

Mouth Health
Oral Health is Very Important

It's difficult to be happy if your mouth is not healthy. The foods we eat not only affect our bodies but they also affect our oral health. We need to take care of what allows us to eat, taste, and nourish our bodies to a healthy happy state.

Ready-to-eat foods are convenient, but perhaps not so much when it comes to your teeth. Eating fresh, crunchy produce not only contains more healthy fiber, but it's also the best choice for your teeth. The bones holding your teeth get a 'workout' when you chew, helping to keep them strong. The saliva produced while chewing is also beneficial, helping to clear food particles from your mouth and wash away bacteria so there may be less plaque buildup and tooth decay.

Achieving healthy teeth takes a lifetime of care. Even if you've been told that you have nice teeth, it's crucial to take the right steps every day to take care of them and prevent problems. This involves getting the right oral care products, as well as being mindful of your daily habits.

Here are some other pointers:

1. Don't go to bed without brushing your teeth

It's no secret that the general recommendation is to brush at least twice a day. Still, many of us continue to neglect brushing our teeth at night. But brushing before bed gets rid of the germs and plaque that have accumulated throughout the day.

2. Brush properly

The way you brush is equally important. In fact, doing a poor job of brushing your teeth is almost as bad as not brushing at all. I bought a highly rated spin brush, "Oral B" so I feel crystal clean each day. There are all kinds of other brands out there, too, that making brushing well much easier than it used to be with only a manual toothbrush.

And don't forget that proper brushing includes the tongue too. Plaque can also build up on your tongue. Not only can this lead to bad mouth odor, but it can also lead to other oral health problems. Gently brush your tongue every time you brush your teeth.

Take care of your tongue by cleaning it and paving the path for clean healthy taste buds, free of bacteria so you can continue to taste yummy things in life.

3. Don't forget to floss

No one, including you, wants to see stuff in between your teeth in your super awesome smile. So flossy flossy, guys!

If flossing seems difficult, rather than give up, look for tools that can help you floss your teeth. Ready-to-use dental flossers from the drugstore can make a difference.

Flossing isn't just to get to those hard to reach places, says Jonathan Schwartz, DDS, "It's really a way to stimulate the gums, reduce plaque, and help lower inflammation in the area."

4. Use mouthwash

Using mouthwash reduces the amount of acid in the mouth, which will bring you closer to your alkaline-based body PH that is healthy.

Health is happy, guys, so let's make sure we are taking a close look and be mindful of the little things that build to be big things.

At the end of the day eating healthy and taking care of our mouths is an easy way to the finish line with a healthy, happy smile for all to see. Our smile is God's gift that shows our happiness, and if our smile is healthy, we are healthy. Especially when you're smiling at yourself in the mirror giving yourself a spunky affirmation and admire that smile while you're at it. It's the gift that keeps on giving so be a giver. It's one of those things that is contagious; smile a lot and most will smile back.

Smiles, hugs, happy! Let's smile a lot even if you might not be happy at the moment; we're working on that. It's super easy to get a good base moving in the right direction.

People with Bad Teeth Vs. People with Good Teeth

It makes me want to turn and run the other way when I encounter people with poor mouth hygiene. I think that if they don't take care of their mouth health, they're probably skimping in other areas of their life also. How we do one thing is often how we do everything. When we encounter something unpleasant, we get an unpleasant feeling from it. I once dated a man who didn't really take care of his teeth, and though I really liked him as a person, he wasn't someone I wanted to kiss, so I didn't. Needless to say, that relationship didn't last long. I'm not proud of making decisions like that, but did you know that gingivitis is contagious?

Yes, it is. According to Harshita Sharma, periodontal surgeon and implant expert, the main source of transmission of bacteria causing gingivitis is saliva. And any kiss that is deep enough to exchange saliva, can transmit gingivitis, too. Harshita notes that one French kiss results in transfer of almost 80 million bacteria. But still the occurrence of gingivitis depends on your own oral hygiene and immunity, too. With time and intimacy, if transmission becomes frequent, your oral bacteria will become more similar as your partner's.

So, make sure to maintain your hygiene properly. It's good to kiss, but kissing with good hygiene is a much better and healthier experience.

It's true: oral hygiene can make you more attractive when dating and with your partner. No one likes to be with someone who doesn't take care of himself or herself. So, remember: healthy food and healthy mouths helps keep a healthy brain and body.

Exercise: Awareness of your Mouth

Once you have spent a few minutes sitting, gently move your attention to your sense of **taste**.

Sense the taste within your mouth, just as it is right now. You might sense sweetness or bitterness, or it could even be a neutral taste. It doesn't matter what the sensation is. Simply rest your awareness of whatever it is that you sense, even if it is a neutral one.

What 3 things that you can taste make you happy? Let's take this time to add notes to our notebooks.

Sense of Smell

"Stop and smell the roses." The expression "stop and smell the roses" is not simply about flowers, but rather about living our lives with deeper appreciation for the world around us. It reminds us to slow down and notice the little things that make life worthwhile. Despite a busy life, it is important to know how to be present in the moment; otherwise, those moments will pass you by. After all, time is our most valued asset.

Why not stop and smell the cookies?

Every time I go into the mall, I smell something good that brings me joy and it's usually the freshly baked Mrs. Fields cookies calling my name. The scent fills the entire mall so you can smell the cookies all throughout and that aroma draws me towards them. Sometimes I'm strong but often I'm weakened by the warm sugar that lures me to purchase and eat them while I shop. Who doesn't like cookies and shopping? I do a lot. Since I'm trying to be good these days, I make sure I have fresh cut fruit on hand daily and some apple cinnamon tea bags. Not only do I get to enjoy the scent of freshly cut oranges, but I am guilt free and being good to myself which is a double win.

I've heard that real estate agents use freshly baked cookies to make the home smell like you live there or want to live there. They're really appealing to you through your senses. Smart people.

But how does your sense of smell work? The sense of smell, just like the sense of taste, is a chemical sense. They are called chemical senses because they detect chemicals in the environment, with the difference being that smell works at dramatically larger distances than that of taste.

Brain centers perceive odors and access memories to remind us about people, places, or events associated with these olfactory sensations. And according to Serene Aromatherapy, "Our sense of smell is 10,000 times more sensitive than any other of our senses and recognition of smell is immediate. Other senses like touch and taste must travel through the body via neurons and the spinal cord before reaching the brain; whereas, the olfactory response is immediate, extending directly to the brain. This is the only place where our central nervous system is directly exposed to the environment."

Is there anything you can remember smelling that has brought you to a settled happy place, a place of relaxation or a place that triggers emotions from where you love to be? There are so many ways to enlighten your sensors through your nose.

When I was young, I would love to go to my grandparents' house and take in the home cooking. I remember from a very young age, before being able to cook myself, sitting up on the counter and watching my grandmother use a rolling pin to flatten her dough. The process behind cooking from scratch is time consuming.

She would craft away in the kitchen, making cookies, baking pies, and during Christmas time she'd make candy. It was pure warm sugar scents all through the house. When my grandmother made fudge, I was waiting for it to settle like a puppy begging for scraps.

I loved cooking with my grandmother and she loved teaching me. The whole smell of breakfast cooking was what I lived for when I went for weekends to my grandparents' house. My favorite memory cooking with grandma was that I got to decide what we made for breakfast in the morning. When I would wake up, I would run into my grandma and grandpas' room and let them know what was on the menu that morning. It was always one of two things: pancakes, eggs, and sausage with syrup and apricot jam or waffles, eggs, and bacon with syrup and apricot jam.

Never anything else. The best time of the day was always when we would prepare the food; smelling and cooking and tasting to be sure it was perfect. That blessed smell of freshly brewed coffee with pancakes and syrup, there's nothing better.

Another scent memory I have is from childhood, when we would wake up early to go fishing with my dad. During those mornings, we hit the road to go fishing and the one thing that I noticed a lot of the time was the morning fog and that clear, fresh smell in the air that caused me to feel alive. Not being a morning person at the time, this was not something I experienced often, so it was a treat. Nowadays, I rise early to enjoy these special feelings like the morning air, sunrises, and the birds singing. But in childhood, we would make it out to the lake and get the real effects from nature. The smell of the water, the trees in the soil, the scent of the fish in the lake all bring good feelings and memories that I want to continue. I find it very pleasurable to smell natural things made by our planet. It's healthy and happy, and it's another way of connecting with our earth.

Do you ever notice how good you feel when you're in nature? Going on a trail hike is one of my favorites because of the smell of dirt and trees. Being so close to Mother Nature brings great peace to our minds. To fill my lungs with the fresh oxygen from heavily wooded areas is a healthy way to connect with your senses. As I walk through the trails being kissed by the sunlight peeking through the trees, I note the natural aromatherapy of the soil beneath my feet. With every breath I take, I feel more at one with myself, like I am supposed to be there. Like it is me. Like I am made of the same compounds. You know, I smell something similar to soil when I make myself a fresh cup of Japanese matcha green tea. For some reason when I smell it and drink it, it reminds me of the feeling I get when I am in nature, probably because I am drinking green leaves. ☒ So, if there is something that you can smell that reminds you of a place that brings peace into your heart, let's take note of those things at the end of this chapter and smell those things more often.

It's a very natural feeling to feel connected to the earth; grounding with the planet adds an instant calm. With each breath the salt in the air naturally soothes the human body because we are 80 percent liquid and so is the earth. Salt water consumes 80 percent of our planet and salted water is in the air, though we just can't see it. Whether we realize it or not, being close to the ocean and breathing heavily salted air of the earth naturally calms the human body. Since I don't currently live on the beach, I have a saltwater humidifier in my room and a Himalayan sea salt lamp so I can try to simulate the ocean while I'm not near it. The salt makes me feel better while I sleep and both things bring a deeper sense of peace during my meditation.

Rain can also have similar effects. Have you ever noticed that sweet smell in the air on the first rain of the season? From what I know, it's from the vehicles dropping motor oil and the rubber from tires on the pavement that has become freshly wet that creates that scent, which triggers me to be relaxed. There's something about the sent in the air that I really love; it helps me be in that moment and take note of what I'm able to smell. In Northern California, it means that winter is here and things are going to slow down quite a bit. We're probably going to gain a couple extra pounds for our winter coat and we're going to be getting more sleep. I also think about soup when it starts to rain and fireplaces. I get a sense of relief that the summer activities have died down and it's time for my winter rest. There is nothing better than a fire crackling in the fireplace for the winter. As soon as I smell the burning wood, it automatically sets my mind into a beautiful wind-down mode. Through my sense of smell a fire will make me happy instantly. I can feel it, see it, hear it, smell it and by golly I can taste it too. Since I am big on being warm, that fireplace fire will make any winter enjoyable for me.

What better treat to add while sitting in front of a fireplace? Why not a warm bowl of soup!

As I've said before, soups are one of my favorites to make and that's partly because I love the aroma and the healing properties soup contains. There's something to be said about staying home on a rainy Sunday, building a fire in the fireplace, and making a huge pot of vegetable soup to eat while vegging out and watching a funny movie. Time to snuggle up to your loved ones, animals, or kids, if you have them, or to your significant other and share with them the joys of a winter home. Anytime is a great time to make new memories.

There's nothing better than the scent of a big pot of soup, chili, or stew simmering on the stove. Or any food for that matter. I'm going to let you in on a great secret to make your winter soup even healthier for all to eat. While chopping your fresh vegetables and herbs, enjoy the healthy aroma from the slicing. Thank yourself, your universe, and your gods for the money to buy this nutritious food to cook for you and your friends to enjoy. Give thanks with every slice of the tomato, with every chop of the onion, and for every tear that onion brings because you are alive. You are able to use your hands for chopping, stirring, and seasoning your food with love. To enjoy this wonderful food, you are preparing to nourish yourself, season your home and everyone who comes, you bless with this warm meal. Pray and bless your food as you prepare and smell it, think good happy thoughts about all of the health it will bring to you and your loved ones. These notes of positivity, blessing, and thanks will allow your meal to bring forth more health and happiness to you and everyone who eats with you. It's like holy water; it will take on a miraculous healing effect. All you have to do is think it, as you cook it. If you have a friend who is ill, make that person some soup and as you make the soup, imagine them getting better and living and enjoying happiness with you. Imagine with every chop, every stir, and every breath, he or she being well and they will be. This is a great way to send healing to others, from your heart and through your food. I know my grandmother was putting out good vibes as she cooked; she may not have realized what she was doing but she was cooking with love always. It works; I know it does! I have an industrial-sized soup pot for those blessed Sundays when I make soup. I make enough to freeze for friends that need my healing soups. I am able to pull a bag out from my freezer and leave it on their door steps. It's the little things that spread happiness and happiness begins with you.

My very favorite meal and time of year has to be Thanksgiving, with the baking of the turkey, the mashing of the potatoes, and the smell of freshly baked pumpkin pie. I also love the smell that emits from a freshly-popped bottle of apple cider as it reminds me of family and a time of celebration. It's another favorite time of year, with the Thanksgiving dinner to enjoy all of my favorite comfort foods with all of my family and friends.

Winter is a lovely time when I enjoy the smell of pine needles, wood smoke, and snow, all clear indicators that winter has arrived. Everything that goes along with winter is what I love most about holidays. All of the aromatic sense of the season: persimmons, apple pies, cinnamon, and fresh vanilla bring joy to almost anybody's soul. Is there anything you love to smell in winter that brings you to your happy place? Take a moment to note it so we can learn how to bring our sense of smell to life all year round!

During winter's chill, the molecules in the air are smaller so there are fewer scents to smell, which makes it a lot more clean, clear, and fresh for us to enjoy the change in seasons. I have a good friend who loves the smell of Christmas trees and every year before Christmas I'll bring him a baby Christmas tree so that way he'll be sure and fill his home with a scents (and sense) of Christmas. Be the gift that keeps on giving. When you bring the gift of scent into someone's life, it begins to have more meaning for them through their senses. Don't forget the sense of smell has the most memory receptors. Now when my friend enjoys the aroma of Christmas, he will think of me also. Another lifelong win-win.

All seasons and times of the year have certain scents. Summer has its own and summer reminds me of Hawaiian flowers, BBQs, campfires, swimming pools, lakes, beaches, and good old-fashioned carnivals. Yep, you know I had to add carnivals, festivals, and theme parks into the summer mix. They always have fun food, drinks, people and warm weather to boot. Just between me and you, they usually have that warm sugar smell that fills the summer air with plenty of cotton candy. But I only consume this now when I'm living a little. ;) We have the ability to capture the aromatic powers of almost any scent naturally. What do you love most about summertime? Is it the waterskiing, hiking, rock climbing, or river rafting? Is it more time in the scent of the ocean? Is it the smell of the woods when you go camping? Or is it a special flower or fruit that is in season?

One flower happens to be my favorite. Anytime I go to the Hawaiian Islands, the puakenikeni is the most memorable of fragrances, because it's a nice blend of floral but not too floral with a full-bodied sweetness to finish. To me, the smell of the Tahitian gardenia flower is the smell of paradise. (This scent can be captured in essential oils but you need to make sure that you get something that's not an artificial fragrance but made from the real thing.) You might have a favorite flower or sent that leave your invigorated present and wanting more. Feel free to make a note whenever something piques your interest. I am looking forward to hearing about how you've turned on your séance of smell to upgrade life experience. A happy person is a healthy, wealthy human.

If I can't be in Hawaii to smell the flowers, I try to simulate it at home with fragrant flowers to freshen my air and bring my environment love because I am worth it. But every time I am in Hawaii, I savor the scent while I'm lying out by the pool or on the beach and taking in the air and what is in it. What about those hot tanned bodies smothered with Tropicana tanning oil that smell like coconuts? Every time I smell that, it reminds me of back in the 1980s when we all used that stuff like it was going out of style and would bake in the sunshine all day to get our deepest tan. I think I will get something that smells like coconut so I can be reminded of the beach in Hawaii while I'm working in my office. I'm going to kick it up a couple notches and throw on some Hawaiian instrumental music to set the tone. I bet I get some awesome writing in being in my environment that touches all my senses ever so perfectly. Our mood is everything. Let's take notes and think about everything we love and make sure these things as not under- used, but over-the-top enjoyed. I can see it now. I'm working at home. I get a visitor. My place smells like Hawaiian flowers, tropical tanning oil. The heater is up to 80, with the sounds of Hawaiian ukulele for back drop music. My miracle of the beach is something to be admired, and I'm wearing a Hawaiian dress. Am I nuts? Nope, I'm simply happy by my own design. If you like it, bring it.

Last night I was walking through Lahaina, Maui, with some friends after dinner and we all commented on the lovely smell of fresh gardenia in the air. I had looked around and noticed we were walking by the tree where the gardenias grow. It's a beautiful scent to remember. I took a panalunini flower and put it in a bottle of water and after 24 hours the water smelt just like the flower, and I had inadvertently made my own spray. Now I will get to smell Hawaiian flowers for the next few weeks at least. I will spray it on my pillow and in my car for sure.

Chemical Reactions

from Smell to Feeling

Olfactory bulbs are part of the limbic system and directly connect to the areas of the brain that process emotion and learning. This is one of the reasons why so often something that we smell will trigger a memory or remind us of something or someone.

Natural smells bring a healing feeling. When we can't be in nature to help remind us we are human beings not human doings, we have a few avenues we can explore. Essential oils are one of them.

Usually steam-distilled or cold-pressed essential oils are extracted from plants, and their medicinal and aromatic properties have amazing benefits. There are thousands of research studies vouching for the remarkable healing and therapeutic benefits of essential oils. Some of the benefits from specific oils and scents include:

Orange with a powerful, uplifting aroma, orange oil has proven benefits for creating feelings of happiness that can improve energy levels. These I would use at a certain time of day when I want to be more alert. For me, morning time is key or even throughout the day while I am at work, creating the best hair ever for my lovely clients.

According to Chinese medicine, lime oil is known to promote energy flow in the body. It works really well for helping you to re-focus and concentrate after working or studying for long hours.

Grapefruit can be added to your shower for a quick energy boost. Add a few drops of grapefruit oil in your shower and cover the drain. Inhale deeply to get the full medicinal benefits. Why not enjoy your shower a little more?

Mint and peppermint have not only been shown to positively improve exercise performance but they can also help improve concentration and fight fatigue. Maybe add a few drops into your water for your workout.

Eucalyptus is an "anti-inflammatory, antioxidant, analgesic," and is also an "immune-stimulatory," according to theconsciouslife.com. Neurological science has revealed that those who suffer from chronic fatigue syndrome have reduced cerebral blood flow, and rosemary oil contains 1.8 cineole and has been shown to increase blood flow to the cerebrum, improving alertness. The oil is also an excellent stimulant and helps fight low energy. A mid-day aromatherapy anyone? Might be a great idea to see which essential oil brings enjoyment and betterment into your life and then engineer the perfect blend into different parts of your day as a way of positively flowing closer to your happy place through your sense of smell.

Thyme has amazing medicinal benefits because it not only positively affects the mood but also helps to reduce stress and lift energy levels.

Basil helps to stimulate the adrenal glands, which makes it excellent for alleviating sluggishness, relieving mental fog, and even fighting chronic fatigue. I add this into the water with strawberry or cucumber slices for my guests at the salon, and people tell me how wonderful they feel when they drink and smell it. Engineering more happiness and health into this beautiful life is at our fingertips and through our senses.

Lemongrass has powerful medicinal healing benefits as it has a fresh, earthy, invigorating scent that instantly uplifts, and can help balance energy and clear the mind. Lemongrass reminds me of Thai food which I love and the essence of it mixed with green tea will give you the feeling your in another part of the world. Adding it to something cool and refreshing like orange infused water is something to experiment with.

Use any of these essential oils to give the room a fresh, airy feeling, to improve your mood, to boost your concentration, to elevate your energy levels, or to be relaxed and sleep well.

Other oils and scents will improve your digestion, lower your glucose levels, and help with depression, so we can say hello to a better life.

Also, you can take a break and have a bath with a few drops of any essential oil to help relax the mind and the body after a long day. Add a few drops to the shower floor to create a spa-like steam room. You are worth it! Take the time and inhale something that brings you a sense of calm. Even taking in deep breaths is God's way of flushing oxygen into the brain so you feel alive and well. Remember to breathe deeply daily because you are alive. I have a sequence of breathing techniques I use to start my day prior to my meditation, which not only wakes me up, but it allows more stress relief to my meditation and allows me to go deeper.

Warm and spicy oils like cinnamon, research suggests, can help regulate blood glucose and combat cravings, irritability, weight gain, and reduced energy levels. Use cinnamon in anything you can, your coffee, your cereal, or even on your toast. In childhood, my brothers and I went through a phase of making cinnamon toast with butter, cinnamon. and sugar. YUM. Love you, my brothers. Next time we get together, your old sis will make you a little surprise treat. With love, of course. I'm excited just thinking about it.

Ginger oil is excellent for maintaining your energy levels. It stimulates the nerves and will keep you pumped to get the job done. Why not add a few drops of any of these into your water? Warm or cold, it's good to ingest, just be sure it is pure in quality. DoTerra and Young Living are reputable brands you can try.

Frankincense essential oil can help alleviate the unpleasant effects of both anxiety and depression while helping boost energy levels. I like to keep a bottle in my car or purse just in case I need to take a deep breath; might as well add something for a little kick in the right anti- stress direction.

Black pepper is known to improve circulation and is excellent to use as a pre-workout essential oil, to promote exercise performance. Peppers of all sorts fire up your metabolism and help you burn more calories. Funny enough, if you smell them in the air, they have a similar effect on your metabolism.

Pine essential oil is excellent for clearing out both physical and mental fatigue. Pine oil invigorates, keeps you alert, and promotes feelings of positivity. This is probably why my friend Brent loves the smell of Christmas trees; there's a positivity factor in there.

Lavender oil can lead to calming down the body and mind. It not only helps in increasing concentration and focus but also improves mood.

Anything we can find these days will add a sense of improved well-being. Note it next time you smell something you love, it will make all the difference in the world.

Cedarwood oil stimulates the pineal gland and the brain's limbic region, which promotes the release of melatonin. This helps you to fall asleep, improves your sleep quality, and makes you feel more energetic the next day. If you know of anyone who has trouble with sleep, forward something like this so they don't need to resort to pharmaceuticals.

My absolute favorite essential oil right now is a blend by Young Living calls Valor. It has been coined first aid for the mind and it sure does the trick. I find myself taking deep breaths of it straight from the bottle at different times throughout the day to help keep me feeling like a million bucks. Everyone I let smell it loves it just as much as I do. It's my secret helper!

Valor essential oil is a blend of Black Spruce, Blue Tansy, Camphor Wood, Geranium, and Frankincense. Valor has a woodsy, grounding aroma that is great for massages and other topical and aromatic uses. I love taking in the Valor. It helps me keep a positive attitude or to refocus at the end of a challenging day; it's an anti-stress at its best.

To help with PMS, hot flashes, menopausal issues, and overall general bitchiness, we use the two oils considered to be the best for those issues: Rose Geranium and Clary Sage. Additionally. Lavender, Bergamot, and Frankincense can all be added because they also have calming properties.

I went to an art and wine festival a few years ago and came across a woman selling essential oil blends. One particular bottle caught my eye because it said the word "bitch" on it. The name of the particular blend was called "spray the bitch away". I immediately thought, oh my god, I'm going to get this for my mother and by golly I'm getting one for myself, too, for those moments when I'm about to blow my lid. What better avenue to take as a safety net than to just "Spray the bitch away."

If you have children who could use a little calming or focus, essential oils are awesome. The companies that manufacture the oils also sell necklaces that hold the scent and release a bit at a time all day and diffusers and personal misters also. My good friend and Chiropractor Dr. Jonathan Means, bought me a diffuser for my car, it plugs into the USB adapter and makes those car rides even more enjoyable. Thank you Jonathan, you are the best!

Why not try them? Essential oils' mood-altering properties are better than using drugs. (Trust me on this as I'm a recovered meth user.) One of the most important lessons I have learned in my life is that the only thing we have control over is ourselves. If you want your house to smell like your favorite spa down the street for that feeling of calm, peaceful tranquility, just ask them what they have in the diffuser and grab one for the house, your new sanctuary.

Diffusers or oils are also super fun gifts. I often spray them on my pillow at night and use them in my car. I have a night mask that I use for travel, and to which I'll add a few drops of my favorite essential oil. And voila! I'm a happy girl, who's blissfully sleeping.

Nature, cooking, and the scent of pure essential oils are way better than any of those artificial cancer-causing fragrances the car wash uses. I don't know about you, but they give me a headache. The things to stay away from are those plug-in room deodorizers and anything like it that's artificial. They can cause headaches and I know they're not good for us. I'm sure I'm not the only one sensitive to them. Here is some shocking but accurate information:

Consumers are being warned that they should rethink modern air fresheners. As researchers have taken a closer look at these seemingly hassle-free devices, they have discovered an astonishing number of toxic compounds are present in many scented gels.

One of the primary concerns health experts have about plug-in air fresheners in their widespread use of phthalates. According to a study conducted by the Natural Resources Defense Council (NRDC), 86 percent of air fresheners tested contained phthalates. Phthalates, which are also found in many plastics, aerosol sprays, paints, pesticides, cosmetics, and fragrances are notoriously disruptive to the body. As the NRDC reports, "Most phthalates are well known to interfere with production of the male hormone testosterone, and have been associated with reproductive abnormalities." Phthalates are on the State of California's list of toxic substances "known to cause birth defects or reproductive harm." The NRDC also warns that airborne phthalates can cause allergic symptoms and asthma.

Even trace amounts of phthalates can accumulate to cause these harmful side effects.

But let's move on to a more positive topic... Body chemistry.

Do we fall in love at first smell?

"Smell" is the woefully inadequate way we describe sensing someone's pheromones — a type of scent-bearing chemical secreted in sweat and other bodily fluids. Pheromones are known to be involved in sexual attraction in animals, and research suggests that they may also play a role for people.

Sexual chemistry identified through our sense of smell is something I'll definitely notice right away if I like somebody or not. Interestingly enough, we are attracted by smell also. I've noticed that the partners in my life have never had a smell I wasn't attracted to. During exercise—whether it be jogging, lifting weights at the gym, doing yoga or ...you know, the horizontal mambo—I've noticed a heightened attraction just from their scent. It's like the icing on the cake. Not only are we attracted to each other's personal looks but the scents take the relationship another step as well, and it may very well be the most deciding factor of compatibility. I've found on the subject of our gift of smell, this is another thing that brings me joy. Any chance I get I take my boyfriend's shirt home with me, especially if he plans to go out of town and I won't be able to see him for a few days. I'll keep his shirt in my bed with me just so I can smell it night and it makes me feel good, makes me feel close to him just through his scent. Our gift of smell continues to give back and keep on giving,

What Three Things Triggers You Happy That You Can SMELL?

What you want to remove   **What you'd love to add**

  1

  2

  3

How will this enrich my life?

Sense of Sight

I opened two gifts this morning; they were my eyes. We should be grateful for so many things and our sight is one of them. Through our eyesight, we have the ability to enjoy our surroundings. Have you ever thought of what it would be like to not have eyes? If your sight were taken from you, you would instantly think of all of the lovely things you enjoyed seeing. I have always taken my gift of sight for granted until the last few years when I learned in the book, *Thank and Grow Rich*, to be grateful for the little things. When I began to become grateful for things like my sight, my hearing, and my ability to walk and talk, there was a shift in my life; suddenly I had more value than ever before. Without our gifts and abilities, nothing else we set out to do or become or acquire would be possible. When I think about my ability to see I realize that it is sight, in part, that allows me to create, dream, or even walk down the street and take in my surroundings. This makes everything shine that much brighter.

Just think of the things we really pray for and are grateful for, like our pets, our children, our significant others, and our homes, just to name a few. Would they even truly be, if it wasn't for our eyes to be able to select those things? In perspective, all of those difficulties or challenges that worry us are really nothing, because we can still see and still choose to "look" at what's more important, like being alive and well and our gift of sight. Circumstances and things are the way they are, but let's not waste time on those things and focus on what we can see for a minute, a day, a week, a month, a year, and for the rest of our lives. The one thing we have control over is ourselves and truly no one else. So, let's appreciate what we see in our everyday lives. Does your home bring you joy? If the answer is no, we have some changes to make. Our homes are one of the most important places for us to love, feel comfort, and enjoy, as they are huge representatives of ourselves. For me, I have always had hand-me-downs and everyone else's stuff in my house, a hodgepodge that never really looked like I wanted it to look. By the same token, I never looked into any home decor or style that appealed to me to understand what sparks joy and what didn't; I was just going with the flow.

But your outside is a reflection of your inside.

It wasn't until I read Marie Kondo's book *The Japanese Art of Organizing* that I began to have a clear sense for what type of decor gives me a good feeling, and I understood that to feel is to heal. Marie Kondo is a genius with her simple, most natural art of loving yourself and your surroundings. It really works. I'm sure her organized home makes her happier, which makes her more successful.

After reading Kondo's book, I began to realize that I loved the feeling I got when walking into a hotel or a staged home. I felt clean, clear, and relaxed in a way I never had in my own living environments. No distractions, no clutter, nothing out of place—exactly the feeling I require when I need focus. Setting myself up for success is multidimensional, and involves my environment including my car, my home, and my office. Everything that I come in contact with in my personal space can and will serve me because it is my choice to make. And yours is your choice to make. There are many aspects that I clearly see in my environment that can help reinforce my focus and not hold me back. After reading Kondo's book and realizing how I felt in hotels, I asked myself, "What is the one thing that distracts me from I want to do?" To help get me closer to my ideal happiness, I decided it was time to get rid of everything and make it look like a hotel with nothing out on the counters but a potted orchid on the dinner table. Simple, for me, is best. Clean and clear is not distracting; it's soothing and that is the main key for most people. I cleared my space, but didn't get rid of everything like I wanted to. I just made it look more like an Airbnb, with no personal effects around. It's less cluttered and I love it.

About three months after I de-cluttered my apartment, my mother called and asked if I'd be willing to get rid of my apartment altogether and move into help my grandmother. I loved the idea, as Grandma and I were very close. When it was time to move, I figured I would get rid of everything since we didn't know how long she was going to be around. I figured it wouldn't be right to spend money on storing things that I wasn't in love with, and most importantly, that I hadn't picked out myself. Funny how the universe works in our favor when we put one foot in front of the other.

After caring for my grandmother until the end of her life, when it was time to get back into another place of my own, and I was thrilled to actually design my own living space from scratch. It was the best thing I ever done for myself besides get the vehicle I really loved. (We will chat about that one later.) I found I really loved the staged homes, clean, clear, airy and modern and that's what I was going to get. I love the color white; it soothes me. After furniture shopping for weeks, I selected a bedroom set that I love. It has a modern white lacquered finish with chrome hardware and the bed has white leather base. It's very posh, if you ask me. When I saw this set in the warehouse, I thought, it doesn't matter what place I put this set it, it will always make me feel sophisticated and fancy, yet very modern, which I love. I was very eclectic before. Everything else I bought fell into place with the bedroom set, because I used it as my inspiration pieces. If it looked good with my inspiration pieces, it would look good no matter what. I have lived in my new home for almost a year now with my new furniture, and every single time I come home I love what I see and it makes my long days at work well worth it. Why? Because that is what I work for: to design my life for what best suits me and best suits my future.

I cannot say enough great things about how your environment and the things you see often and focus on can help you grow. Our environments can either suck the life out of us or give us life. If your environment is sucking your life, change it. Your quality of life depends on it.

Is there something you'd like to see that makes you feel good, some things that make your work day well worth it? Many people love a multitude of different things and that is why it's your design to do; there's only one for you.

When we are in mindful states, everything works to our advantages and brings more of our minds to us. Awakening our

69

subconscious activates our special abilities and connects us to the universe, and the way to do this is actually an easy trick. It's as simple as being grateful for the little things that are actually the bigger things, like our gift of sight. Being able to see things that make you happy is a gift in itself; not only can we see to drive and walk, but we can see other things that trigger our happy endorphins. What do you see that makes you happy? Do you have a special photo of someone you look up to that makes you happy every time you look at it? Is there a movie you like to watch that always makes you laugh? Or is there a funny quote or joke that gets you every time? Those are happy moments and we can use these to fill our tanks today. I was on a call this morning with my accountability teammates and we always do an awareness exercise as a reminder every day. Today was about how small we are in the universe and in our world, that we are just one person of many. We can be individuals doing only things for ourselves or we can bring ourselves outward into the community by working as a team and making a difference. We spoke about legacy and what would we could leave behind? We asked each other, "How would you be remembered?"

Stop reading for a moment now and find something to smile about, whether it is your son or daughter's face that brings light into your life or your significant other, your cat or dog, someone famous who you love who brings you joy. Simply print out a photo and put it somewhere you can see it every day, and smile away, and have a great day.

What do you see in your personal surroundings on a daily basis that could help stimulate your happiness? Since I can't be in Hawaii at the drop of a hat, I need improvise and create my space.

I wear Hawaiian dresses; I have a tan and wear pineapple coconut perfume. My home decor reminds me of Hawaii. My home's soundtrack is Hawaiian lounge music. My houseplants are palm trees, and I keep the heater on or the fireplace going since I love to feel the warmth. My walls are filled with murals of tropical plant settings, sunsets, and ocean views. I eat Hawaiian foods including some poke, seaweed salad, fruits, and anything coconut. By doing this I have designed my happy place: Hawaii at home! And why not throw in a hot cabana boy fanning me with a leaf? Shazam!

What would you like to see in your personal space that would make you feel like your best self? The more books I read, the more I am encouraged to dream wild and fantasize with my best imagination possible about what I set out to do and who I want to become. What will be supportive and reflect these thoughts? We can take those thoughts and use them as building blocks and turn them into the real thing. Do you ever get that sense of fear in your gut or a feeling that you're not good enough when you see something you want or like, but quickly look the other way because you're afraid of taking that step? Or think you couldn't get it? Or don't know how to attain it? My thought is we need to add more value and empowerment into our personal space and treat ourselves like we are who we want to become right now. Because we are so worth it! When we continue and get used to treating ourselves selfishly, we realize we are worth our best life and won't hesitate to go after these real things we want all the time. All we have to do is think about what makes us feel alive and do it. So, let's break outside this normal mediocre box and into something that gives us worth and helps us feel our real true selves.

What makes you feel great when you look at it? Let's relive and take note of some place you've been that had an impact on you, to where you said, "Wow! That is nice, I want one of these!" What colors bring you joy? Which style of decor speaks to your soul? What could you do to your home that would make you feel like this is your best life ever? Treat yourself. If you have always walked through a door that you don't like, change it. If you sit in a chair that is uncomfortable, buy a new one. The little things make a difference.

What if your place of business felt like you were on a vacation at the same time? That would be cool. Does your workspace make you feel creative, focused, or distracted? And what about your vehicle? When you see it, does it excite you? Be sure it suits your future self.

Art, color, and design have been proven to make people happy. Christopher Thorstenson, of the University of Rochester, ran a set of experiments that were designed to test just how strongly emotions color the world around us. The results of those experiments showed that red is associated with power, energy, warmth, love, and strength. If you want to feel empowered bring some red into your life. Blue is the color of the sky and the ocean, which can make us feel easy and calm. If a room is colored grey and blue or green, you might fall flat and feel dull, slow, very relaxed, and/or depressed. Any earthy colors like the color of dirt, trees, or pavement have a settled normalcy to them that is familiar. I would call these neutral colors, not happy and not sad just easy on the eyes. Yellow is typically a color associated with happiness Any variation of yellow, orange, or reds help you feel more upbeat. Accenting with neutrals would be the middle ground of ease. Anything in the darker family would create a diminishing feeling. In the art of color, dark makes things look smaller, that's why the saying that black clothing is slimming rings true.

When I think of art, I think color, creative flow, design, and a way to get out of my own head and into something that makes me happy.

What is art to you? Anything can be art, including us. What kind of art appeals to you? People collect art as an investment, but what about art that purely brings on a smile or a feeling, something that allows us to feel love and warmth when you look at it. Bridget Watson Payne, in *How Art Can Make You Happy*, writes about the reaction we get from looking at art and how it brings magic into our lives. When researchers hooked people up to EKG's and then the people looked at art, the part of the brain that lit up is the motor cortex, which controls the movement in the body. This means we actually feel art in our body not just in through our eyes and into our brains; art affects all of our receptors and leads to a deeper connection with ourselves and our world. Art helps us be in the moment and appreciate that there are beautiful things around us. When you see something that brings the moment to a standstill, I suggest, bringing that item into your personal space where you can make time stand still over and over again and evolve. It's like seeing a movie for the second time; we hear and see things we didn't the first time. It's time to enjoy the view around us. Small pieces of enjoyment lead to a much greater appreciation with the grand view.

I received a fortune in my cookie and it read: A journey of 1,000 miles begins with one small step. I posted this on my vision board to remind me that to get to our end result of happiness, if that's what it is, we must take tiny steps in that direction. Reading this book is a first step and taking more to get to your 1,000 miles requires not just reading this book, but taking action in learning yourself and what brings you joy. Fill every moment with whatever that might be. Each step should bring joy. If it doesn't, you are going in the wrong direction.

Just as seeing is our gift and a way to make us happy, taking a break from seeing is also a gift and very useful. Closing our eyes helps us clear the unnecessary noise (and allows us to "see" it as such). The saying "our eyes are the gateway to the soul," has new meaning for me now. Our soul is behind our eyelids, doors we can close anytime we choose. It is our choice to shut down and retreat to our sanctuary, to close the door to the outside world. We can go into this private sanctuary that no one else can see, but us. Our mindset or reset can protect and rejuvenate the way we process ourselves and the world. Our mind is our teacher, we just need to sit, see, listen, and be.

One way we can see our inner selves is by closing our eyes and meditating. By looking inward, we can better understand ourselves and what makes us happy. And meditating and looking inward has health benefits, too. According to a Carnegie Mellon University study that was published in the journal *Biological Psychiatry*, meditation and mindfulness may help reduce inflammation, thus lowering the risk of such inflammatory diseases as cancer, diabetes, and Alzheimer's.

Approximately half of the study's participants attended a three-day mindfulness meditation retreat, while the other half attended a three-day relaxation retreat whose regimen did not include mindfulness meditation. The researchers collected and studied blood samples from each participant before the retreats and four months afterward. The subjects who completed the mindfulness meditation program were found to have lower levels of the inflammatory health biomarker interleukin 6 than the participants who attended the relaxation retreat.

One of Carnegie Mellon's researchers, Adrienne Taren MD/PHD said, "By modulating functional connectivity, you're affecting the cell groups that influence the release of inflammatory markers and stress hormones."

Meditation has been proven to reduce our inflammation and gives us a superpower ability to recover quickly from stressful situations. Just by closing our eyes and taking a break, we can process quickly and efficiently.

Sitting in silence also helps IBS and digestive relief, the easing of cold symptoms, and helping to regulate blood pressure. Meditation was even shown to beat morphine in reducing pain.

It even helps you look younger. It's a win-win, in my book. Closing our eyes and meditating is even more beneficial in today's society. Take for example that during a 30-minute evening news segment, your eyes watch 24 minutes of negative garbage news and 6 minutes of commercials, where you are inundated with messages that you are not good enough, that you are not happy, that you need pharmaceuticals. All of these things we take in through our eyes (and ears) are subconsciously programing our minds for unhappiness.

We see commercials for all kinds of burgers and tacos and fries. The fast food industry is a trillion-dollar industry advertising an unhealthy life for you. Doesn't that look juicy and make you hungry? Just watching these commercials actually releases chemicals in our brain that make us want it. Fast food is not healthy. If you have a problem with consuming an abundance of unhealthy foods, stop watching TV for a while and positively reinforce your ability to stay away from the unhealthy and read something to scare you in a healthy direction. The industry gets paid to make you sick so you go to the hospital and stay in their money-generating funnel.

What we unknowingly program ourselves to be insecure, depressed and need to be something that we are not to feel good about ourselves.

People and Social Media

Let's take a moment and think about other things you see, like social media influencers. Are these people giving you, your children, your friends and family the wrong impression of what's cool or what you are supposed to be? I think some might be. Please beware of what you are watching and whom you are following. Take a step back and ask why am I following this person? What am I learning? How is this person benefiting my life and bringing joy into it?

Ask these questions about the people in your immediate circle as well because we see them, and become more like them; it's our nature. Please take the time to really see the people you look up to and ask yourself: Is this person going to get me further from or closer to my goals?

We are influenced by expensive cars, high-priced clothing, and a jet-setting lifestyle. It's all reality TV and publicity to get you to spend more money on brands. Simply being aware of it in a healthy way will make you a happier person. Is watching this going to help you with your life accomplishments? Questioning yourself is always good. Questions are thought-seeds that grow. After all, our choices pave our paths and people do not really decide their futures; they decide their habits and their habits decide their futures.

Influencers can keep us from being grateful for what we do have and keep us further from who we are and our purpose Write a list of 5 things you are grateful for; I'm sure it will elevate your mood.

About three years ago, my realizations of what I was filling my mental space with was terrifying. So, I did the unthinkable and removed both of my televisions from my house. I sold those puppies.

Removing my televisions was one of the healthiest things I could have done for myself. On my list of what I was going to remove was the TV, and what I would use as a substitute was to read books instead.

Why not choose healthy programing that makes ourselves stronger and cherishes our gift of life. We can become closer to knowing who we are meant to be by spending more time meditating and reading self-improvement and other nonfiction books. Through those, our purposes will be revealed.

So, I read with my gift of sight.

Out to the Movies

Since I removed my televisions from my home, it gives me opportunities to enjoy movies of my choice at the theatre. I always opt for the feel-good type of movies. The other day I was at my friend Mike's house. We both wanted to watch *The Mule* with Clint Eastwood. Since we weren't able to see it at the theater, we streamed it. As I started watching the movie, I got so anxious that I voiced the words, "I don't like this movie." I had anxiety for the next three days and it wasn't until two and a half days later that I realized it was the after-effects to my nervous system from the movie. Our bodies will always let us know when something isn't good for us, if we choose to listen and make a healthy choice. Next time that happens, I'm going to excuse myself and do something else. It's not worth the shock to

my system. After all, it's my design and happiness.

Dating Sites

Other places we see things that may affect us include dating sites and apps. Swipe right or left anyone? Dating sites can ruin our self-esteem and what does swiping do to our minds? These apps are programing us to be more and more insecure as the days go on. And slowly but surely, we become addicted to abuse and feel empty without it.

The Gift that Keeps on Giving

Other times we see things that feel like they speak to our souls...or at least give us over-the-top joy. I was in the mall one day and I saw these Doc Marten combat boots from across the mall. They caught my attention because they were different: all black sequined and the sequins changed colors from black to silver when you swiped them. I thought, wow! Those are really cool. They were visually bringing me joy. So, I tried them on and they were super-duper cool. I felt a big YESSS inside myself. I'm a hairdresser so these are right up there in the platform artist realm for me so I bought them. Things that bring me joy like that usually bring others joy also. And every time I wear them, people smile, and they strike up conversations. These boots are the gift that keeps on giving. I've got clients that come in and the first thing they see are these awesome sauce shoes and they're like "wow. Those are so cool." Needless to say, it's a great fun day every time I wear them.

I love seeing fun things and other people's happiness. For example, I was at the airport take a flight to Hawaii to finish this book when I decide to make a pit stop to the ladies' room. Right when I walked in, I noticed a woman with pink hair, a fluorescent yellow hat, a camo windbreaker, and these really awesome rhinestone combat boots. She was super cute and her appearance was screaming happy and fun. This brought me joy just looking at her. Things like this make me smile, and I'm sure they make other people smile, too. Since she appeared so outwardly open and inviting, I struck up a conversation with her. I said, "Oh my gosh, cute boots!" I told her they must bring her joy every time she puts them on just because they look so dang exciting. I explained it must be like going to a disco every single day when you're wearing them. She told me they were her favorite shoes and I can see why.

Things like this remind me of when I like to wear colored wigs and dress up in fun costumes for the whole entire month of October because it's more acceptable then. Halloween is definitely one of my favorite holidays. What I've observed is every time I'm wearing something fun, whether it be a colored wig or some spunky funky shoes, people walk by and smile. More often than not, complete strangers say something nice and strike up conversations because they feel compelled to. Humor and fun are two of the best things to help people put their guards down.

Wig Wednesdays

Because of this, I created Wig Wednesday when I was taking care of my grandmother. Years back, two days after Halloween was over, I didn't want it to end. I wished Halloween was all year long so it would be okay and acceptable for people to dress up in costume any day they liked and it wouldn't be weird. I love costumes. I love making them and I love wearing them. I truly feel like I am in the zone when I'm doing things like this. Anything crafty is fun for me.

When I was living with my grandmother, I always like to do fun things with her, like smoking candy cigarettes after dinner or doing fun face masks for beauty night. But one of my most favorite times was wig Wednesdays when we would both put on fun colored wigs. This was really fun for her and me because we simply enjoy each other's company.

She suffered from dementia so she didn't remember what she even had for lunch even an hour later, so I figured every moment needed to be fun and exciting for her.

When I decided to start wig Wednesdays, it was to do something fun and exciting with my grandmother so that way when my mom came to relieve my morning shift so I could go to work, she would be surprised that my grandmother was all dressed up sitting in her chair with a fun colored wig on, matching earrings, and lipstick, of course.

Grandma love being well dressed.

One morning, something from the day before had me feeling a little down that day. While I was getting ready for work that Wednesday morning, I was resisting the day. It was gloomy outside and it crossed my mind to cancel all of my clients and take a personal day (which I never do). I walked into the den where I kept my jackets (at Grandma's house), and I looked up and saw all of my awesome colored wigs where I display them on the shelf, then I realized it was Wednesday, wig Wednesday. I instantly got happy and went straight for the wigs because it was a fun day and playtime no matter what the circumstances. As I decided what wig I was going to wear (I've got all kinds, pink, blue, red, Ombre, and a curly one that's from my Cher Halloween costume) I thought, thank God, it's wig Wednesday. Oh, now I'm really excited. Anything that could have been making me sad that day was suddenly gone.

So, every time I need a little cheering up, I throw on a wig and look at myself in the mirror. I have fun with it, and throughout the day of wearing the wig everybody who sees it smiles about it, too.

One time my girlfriend Maggie had rallied me and two of her other girlfriends to go and serve fireball shots at an event for her boss' birthday. I thought, why not dress up as "fireball girls"? So, we donned the 22-inch flaming red wigs, black dresses, and red fishnet tights; we were the talk of the town. Boy, did we have fun! Dressing up for fun gives a happy-go-lucky sense of sight we love to see in ourselves, but it's a gift we give to everyone around. We should do this every day!

So have fun. Do something that you get to look at and that brings you joy, and chances are it will bring joy to those around you as well.

Your sense of sight is the gift that keeps on giving.

Look at yourself:

Is there something you'd like to see that brings you joy?

Why not walk over to the mirror right now and embrace your beauty? Many women I have come across do not practice self-care because they think it's selfish when they have families to care for and they always put themselves last. They are not in the habit of being good to themselves, and then they end up not seeing any value within themselves.

I once wrote a letter to my female clients to help them see and understand the impact of self-care can have on us. It was really beautiful.

I will enclose it here for anyone who might need a reminder

of how awesome you are and how fun life is with you in it. (And while it was written to my female clients, the information is equally applicable to any gender.)

Good Morning, Beautiful Woman of the World!

It's a lovely day out on the town today and there are so many awesome things you are going to do. The most fun part of the whole thing is that YOU will be there, shining like the bright star that you are. You are a lovely soul. I'm really excited to hear about the many gifts and opportunities that find you in your day. When you get up today before you choose your gorgeous clothing, I'd like you to walk over to the mirror for a moment. I want you to look at your face, your hair, and into your eyes deeply and say, "I love you." Take a good look at your reflection; what you are looking at right now is what can only be a miracle. Yourself, your body, your heart beating to give you life and opportunity is nothing to be taken for granted. Look into your eyes. Your eyes see your beautiful self and they see the people you love, the world around you, and these are things to be thankful for, in addition to your nose that you can breathe through and bring oxygen into your lungs, your brain, and your blood. Take a deep breath right now. One big one in.... and let it out.

You are a gift to yourself. You are a gift to the world, your colleagues, your family, your friends, and the passerby who don't know you yet.

While you are preparing yourself for your day today, think of these moments as though you are preparing for the best day of your life. Think about all of the people you would love to meet in your life and how you would hope to look when you encounter these people.

What will you be wearing? What is the style of your hair? A piece of flare, today? It is a celebration of your life. Think of today as an exciting day!

The world will be blessed with your presence. You are happy, bright, and beautiful. As you prepare yourself as the gift that you are, do it with a smile. Put on your favorite music while you prepare yourself to greet your day. These precious moments when a woman has to polish and rejuvenate herself for herself is ceremonial. This is your time to make sure you shine and feel great inside yourself.

Before you leave your house today, walk over to the mirror again and look deep into your eyes and say, "I can have anything I desire and I am going to have the best day of my life."

Thank you for being you. I love you.

Seeing Words of Affirmation

In my car on the inside of my visor right next to my mirror I have a little piece of paper and printed on it reads the words, "You're worth it."

Every time I go to open the mirror so take a look at myself I read those words and remember that I'm worth it and this is my reminder for special care. Often times we need reminders to care for ourselves and to have fun.

I find affirmations very important as a way of reminding ourselves, all over our homes, in our vehicles, and at work, of our prize. To continue building ourselves up each and every day, affirmations are free ways to add value and raise our personal stock. How much is your personal stock worth? 100 million dollars? I think so!

What three things trigger you happy that you can SEE?

What you want to remove   **What would you love to add?**

1

2

3

How will each thing enrich my life?

Sense of Sound

The fourth way we can design ourselves a happier life is through our sense of hearing. Sound means to make a noise. And the truth is, most people can hear, but few people choose to listen. But let's delve deeper into what sound is and how our sense of hearing works and how we can use this sense to create a happier, more positive environment for ourselves. So, let's begin with the basics.

What Sound Is

Sound is energy that simply travels in waves. These waves are vibrations where the air particles hit against each other until they reach the inner ear causing the ossicles bones to vibrate and send information to the brain via the auditory nerves.

How Your Ears Work

The ear is a very complicated organ made up from tiny bones, tubes, and membranes that allow you to hear sounds. To put it simply, when the moving molecules enter your ear, the pressure behind them causes the tiny bones to move.

The Science Behind How Sound Affects Us

The human voice is one of the most powerful sounds on the planet. It's the only sound that can encourage us or even start a war. Hearing is our primary warning sense. Whether it's a sudden cold sweat caused by a snake's warning hiss, or the uncontrollable grin as your favorite song plays on the radio, our ears provide us with information.

Sound affects our body in four different ways: physiologically, psychologically, cognitively and behaviorally.

Physiologically, sound affects our bodies. Your body is 70-percent water. Sound travels well in water, so we're very good conductors of sound.

Psychologically, sound can change our emotions and our moods. Music will do it, affirmations, and even a good podcast can change our moods. I'm sure you can think of a song that will make you happy. Listening to a favorite genre, even thinking of mine right now—country music—puts me at ease.

Cognitively, how well you concentrate is dependent on the sounds around you. The most distracting sound of all is the human voice. In cognitive psychology, people's susceptibility to distraction by background sound or noise is often used as an instrument to understand the nature of selective attention and short-term memory. Many theories have been proposed to explain why people tend to perform better in silence compared with when there is noise present in the background.

Behaviorally, we tend to move away from unpleasant sounds if we can and gravitate towards more pleasant sounds. Let us move from honking horns from the city commuters towards the country where we can hear the birds singing.

Sound affects us in four direct ways; let's start to design our environments so that those effects are not working against us. We need to be aware that sound is associative; we associate certain emotions and even thought with certain sounds.

Do we ever stop to think how lucky we are to be able to hear things? Take a moment right now and really listen. What sounds do you hear? Can you hear the low hum of your refrigerator? The rustle of the leaves on a tree outside your window? Are you sitting in front of a fireplace, listening to the fire? Can you hear a car's tires on the pavement or a truck's engine idling nearby? Our ears take in so many things in every second, things we aren't consciously aware that we are processing.

Other things we should be more conscious and selective in hearing. I was reading a book one day after a good friend, Neil, lent it to me because I was feeling down and out. Yes, it was a break-up, which took my security blanket right off and left me with myself. The book is over 40 years old, older than me, was published in the early 1970s and it is titled, How to Be Your Own Best Friend, by Mildred Newman and Bernard Berkowitz. As I read the book, an interesting short story had me more engaged than I had ever been in my entire life while reading anything. It was about the glow you get from words of affirmation, but it wasn't about the ones you hear from yourself. The lesson in how to be your own best friend was about the affirmations you hear from other people. Being instantly intrigued, I learned that there was a huge difference between getting an affirmation from yourself as opposed hearing them from others. The realization triggered something inside of me that gave me a cross between butterflies and a wrench to my gut, kind of like going down in an elevator really fast. I was excited and terrified at the same time. My eyes opened wider, my senses were heightened, like I was going to start an internal recording. In that moment I felt like I could have a photographic memory and that I was never going to forget what I was about to read.

The example was about the world's most marvelous performers. The whole time leading to the performance, these professionals are filled with self-doubt and zero recognition that they are doing well. All of their discipline and all of their training just to wait until the end of the performance.

The end of the performance was the time to receive a lifetime of satisfaction and recognition. When the show is over, these performers would gauge their personal level of accomplishment by the sound of the clapping coming from the crowd. How long they clapped, the expressions on their faces, their body language and whether or not there was a standing ovation. The crowd would be read and analyzed for recognition of how great he or she performed.

At the end of the show, most performers were so happy from the roars of the crowd; it lifted them right off their feet allowing their spirits to soar high like a kite.

As they floated back to their fitting rooms, the glow from the crowd began to fade. Almost as soon as they shut their dressing room doors, they were cold as ice and right back to where they started. To my surprise, the performers were cold, empty, and completely alone all over again. When the self-confident happy meter was gone, so were they. That's no way to live. The story went on to explain that these world-famous performers never heard how great they were from themselves. When we don't hear it from ourselves, then we can become a prostitute to the opinion of others.

That's probably why many don't go on to do what they dream of doing, because they will be judged and if it's not great, good luck to you. Could you imagine how terrible it would be if the crowd thought your performance was shit? I'd hate to think of where that might leave someone.

I'm sure all of us have fallen victim to this kind of self-treatment. This lesson is without a doubt the prime example of someone who does nothing for himself but everything for other people. You may have heard similarities in the term referenced as "people pleasing". Crippling, isn't it? It's not that the performers didn't have minds of their own; it's simply they didn't know how to use them to build belief within themselves. I have a sign on my wall just in front of the foot of my bed as a reminder. It reads, "Start each day with a grateful heart." Just in case I forget, I will see it. I go to bed seeing this reminder, too.

The moral to this story is to celebrate every step of the way because we all put in efforts daily, and daily we deserve to be celebrated by our own voices and heard by our own ears. The thought of great men/women putting their lives success, progress, and accomplishment into the hands of others for approval is one of the most saddening things to see. I could speculate that this is why so many become close to the end of the rope because they don't know how valuable they are before they set out to do great things. Could you imagine if your son or daughter was putting himself or herself into a role of self-inflicted emotional abuse? I have done it to myself for years, and that is why this story hit home for me.

So many people fall victim to selling themselves short in the world, especially with social media on the rise. With YouTube, Instagram, and Facebook likes, many people gauge their personal value through their online following. Every day you need to tell yourself how you are one of the greatest achievements. Be that secretly arrogant person who walks around unharmed by how people evaluate you. You evaluate yourself, every day, and tell yourself that you are great, even if you don't think you are; you will become great by telling yourself. This message is incredibly important for you to hear.

How I Started Affirmations

It's time to turn this ship around. The best time to tell yourself how fabulous you are is when you are in front of the bathroom mirror in the morning and at night while brushing your teeth. Talk to yourself and look deep into your own eyes. What I am about to teach you comes from three years of experience with affirmations, learning about them, reading them, writing them, and saying them aloud. I know what they can do and what they will do when you speak your handcrafted words to yourself.

A little over three years ago I felt it necessary to try something new in my life. At the time, I was a status quo hairdresser, with more potential in her pinky finger than she was giving herself the opportunity to be. I didn't know what I was going to do, but I was going to clean up my act and see what this life is really all about, and most of all, who I really was in my core. I told myself when I would give it my all by trying my hardest to be all I could be, and if it didn't show results, I would go back to my regular "party girl" lifestyle. So, the next day, I quit drinking, smoking, and doing drugs, which were my normal staples for something "fun to do". I had faith that if I started there, the rest would come, and it did.

A few months after my act was clean, I was in search for more. I randomly met a woman whom I would have never met before, had I not been on a different path. She gave me the book that would soon change my life forever. I told her I had been clean and sober for the last two months and have been enjoying yoga as something healthy to do in my newly found spare time. I had been really wanting to get into yoga because of the spiritual benefits, and I heard that is helps our posture also. I needed to take care of my body so I could continue to do hair for a long time, and so I needed to get better at yoga. I showed up at Peacebank Yoga Studio in Redwood City, California, not far from where I lived. Peacebank was one of the only places that had a 6 a.m. class all the way across the board Monday thru Friday and a 7 a.m. class on Saturdays and Sundays. I knew that since I was in charge of shaping my life the way it needed to be for my success, becoming an early bird was high on the list. If I were to be able to force myself to get to yoga class, I would be 10 steps above the rest, but I would have to get there first. I wanted to be the greatest hair stylist of all time, and I knew being the early bird that gets the worm would be one of the ways to get there.

The woman I met told me that I needed The Miracle Morning. I said, "the Miracle what?" She said, "The Miracle Morning! Don't worry I have a brand-new copy for you; I will give it to you tomorrow."

I couldn't imagine what could possibly be in this book and that its contents could get me to be a morning person. I couldn't wait for the next day. I believed what she said, as she was about 20 years older than me and seemed very knowledgeable about life and business.

The next day we met to lay out in the sun where she gave me the book. The cover had a man on the front with his hands up looking into the sunrise, like a god. I started reading. I read the story about Hal and what brought him to his rock bottom to where he threw his hands up and he was ready to do anything to change the way he felt in his life. I was about two chapters in, and I got the notion of the five daily savers (a morning routine) and 10 minutes of each and you were a new person. I dog-eared the page, got a piece of binder paper, and wrote my guided list for what to do. I woke up at 5 a.m. the very next day, July 11, 2016, the first morning I started my savers, yoga, and the beginning of my affirmations.

I knew I needed something great, and this was the greatest thing I had ever experienced. The Miracle Morning, by Hal Elrod, was where I started to learn about how to use affirmations to program myself. I started by writing them for 10 minutes in a journal every day. I wasn't used thinking about all the reasons why I was so great, so it took months to begin to get good at it. I ended up in a full-fledged fairytale land within myself that I was some super hero who could do and was doing great things. I was going off: I am the greatest hair stylist that ever lived and people would fly from all over the world to see me and have me do their hair, because I was the best! Between you and me, this is beginning to happen. And so, you couldn't imagine the things I am saying to myself now, a few years later.

Eventually I grew in my affirmations practice and started saying them aloud, and then I evolved to saying them to myself in the mirror, which was even better. This is where things got real. That old fairytale popped into my head, "mirror, mirror on the wall, who's the fairest of them all?" After all this was "my miracle morning" and I could do and experiment with whatever I wanted. I started repeating my affirmations aloud to myself. This felt about as foreign as they did when I started writing them, and then I evolved into having fun with it! The sky is the limit, so don't limit yourself in what you say. These things begin to happen. Repeat the same thing daily and they will begin to happen. After they happen, you cross them off and replace them with the next thing you desire. Don't think this is a bunch of hocus pocus, it's as real as you are. Your words are your wand!

Come up with three simple affirmative statements to start telling yourself regarding how cool you are and how much you rule at being you. You know Adam Levine and Behati Prinsloo's his and hers tattoos that read "you're so cool, you're so cool"? Every time they read it on one another they know it's a reminder, just like my sign when I wake up in the morning. Be even more affirming and say the words aloud; remember your words build your power. I just love seeing affirmations anywhere that remind me how powerful I am. In my car driver's seat visor, every time I flip it down, I see the words "you are worth it" and I say this aloud as I look in the mirror. Affirmations aren't just to read; you bring them to life when you hear them out loud. This might feel foreign at first, but I promise you will become a natural at it and everyone around you will be happy when they hear you saying great things to yourself. This will be the gift that keeps on giving. If we all start now and get used to saying affirmations, everyone will be doing and saying wonderful things and we will see firsthand how powerful it will be.

Also, when you catch yourself saying something negative, which we all do, counter that by saying aloud three things you are grateful for and it turns right into a positive. This might only take you one minute to do so, but do it. It will change your frame of thought ricochet into your life and begin to lift you up. When we are elevated, we tend to lift and elevate those around us too. The real challenge with negative talk is when you catch yourself thinking something negative; make sure you still voice three great things to condition those thoughts right out of your head. Old programing from negative self-talk isn't doing us any favors. Let's push ourselves forward into the people we want to become.

How to Train Your Sense of Sound Through NLP

NLP stands for Neuro-Linguistic Programming. Neuro refers to your nerves and sense organs system. Linguistic refers to language, and programming refers to how that neural language functions. And our programming is how we condition ourselves by the things we do or think or hear repetitively. Neuro-Linguistic Programming shows you how to take control of your mind with your voice, and therefore your life. Unlike psychoanalysis, which focuses on the why, NLP is very practical and focuses on the how.

What I love about NLP is that the approach provides practical ways in which you can change the way that you think, view past events, and approach your life.

In other words, learning NLP is like learning the language of your own mind. Every time you hear your own words go from your mouth and back into your two ears, it's full circle positive reinforcement that soaks into each of your cells. The first time I ever heard of the term of NLP I was having a conversation with a hair client. She referred to herself as a doctor of the mind. She helps her clients with their mental well-being and trains them to leave fear at the door. She was a type of life coach with counseling credentials. She was a really cool lady, very uplifting and a seemed very open and aware of the world when it comes to people. She was also clairvoyant and spiritual. We were talking about affirmations and I had mentioned my morning affirmation that I, at the time, was writing in my notebook for ten minutes as a routine for my Miracle Morning. I was really excited about them and how much they were helping. She asked me if I knew anything about Neuro-Linguistic Programming. She explained that our cells in our brains and bodies could be activated and programmed with whatever we want.

I was fascinated by this conversation and I was going to put it to the test that night. I went straight to my computer in the back breakroom at work and quickly typed up everything she told me. Then, I typed up a quick affirmation to listen to for the first time on my way home that night. And I couldn't believe my ears, there was my voice telling myself great things, on my car speakers like I was listening to someone famous. I felt my shit-eating grin and I had to capture it by looking in the mirror. I almost couldn't believe my ears. This was great, the greatest actually. The feeling really got into my core.

The next day I started recording audio clips for things like affirmations before dates and things to listen to before work. I started listening to my own self tell me how my day was going to play out. Literally I was taking it to a fairytale land level and it was a fantastic feeling. Listening to your own voice on stereo as you drive to work is programing your cells to expect all of the great things that were about to happen. I even began to recording things for other people for more practice. My friend Marc moved to the Silicon Valley to raise $10 million for his start up. Every time he spoke of the grueling days he was having, I thought I would never want that job. It seemed as if his life depended on attaining this outrageous amount of money, and listening to him, I thought, how in the world is he going to make this happen? So, I gave the best advice I knew how to give; I started from the top. Like my mastermind Jarvis Leverson says, "Win your morning and you win your day!" I explained that if he woke up early to program himself and exercise, the second he hit the door that morning he would have 50 percent more energy, brainpower, and confidence than anyone else he came in contact with. And the one thing I knew for sure being in the beauty business is people trust you when they see something they like. I promised him he would have the feeling of Superman and just with his energy alone would have the right words and the perfect body language to win the heart of anyone he faced, so much that it would be unfair for his opponent. I had to say no more; he was in. There was only one problem: Marc wasn't accustomed to waking up early. He saw that as the only thing standing in his way. When I presented him with a solution of a morning affirmation wake up voice clip specifically made just for him, he looked at me with disbelief and said that would be some trick. So, I said, let me take a swing at it.

I thought, what would a man need to start his day through his sense of sound? What's the one thing a man would want every morning when he opened his eyes? What do men like? I thought of many things that would surely get him excited, like fishing, hunting, shooting, and fighting. I've dated my fair share of men, and to my knowledge the only thing I know that might have a sure-fire way to get a heterosexual man marching is a hot woman. I asked Marc to tell me about his childhood crush. Cameron Diaz. Okay, no problem, Cameron Diaz it is. So I started some sexy talk to lift the spirits, in a PG-13 type of way. "Good morning, Mr. Handsome Pants. It's time to get up and build your perfect day because the most exciting things are going to happen today. Cameron Diaz will be waiting at The Woodside Bakery at 9 a.m. (his favorite Bay Area breakfast place) to help start your day off right. You don't have much time so get to the gym; she likes big muscles so go pump some iron this morning. And she will be wearing a red dress, your favorite color, so don't forget to put on your best shirt. Kiss kiss, sexy man. She's waiting."

I sent it off to Marc and no more than one minute later, he phoned me back. "Wow, you've done this before." Needless to say, Marc has been using this new alarm clock method for good luck for quite some time. Over the course of the new few weeks, he even signed his deal for $10 million.

It's great to have friends who are willing to help you with a fun audio clip. And though I have been making recordings for a while now for other people, affirmations are always better coming from your own lips and going back into your own ears. So many people listen to guided mediations and guided affirmations that are generic. Now it's time to hear what you want from yourself. Your sense of sound and your voice are yours to use.

In fact, go ahead right now and think of the one thing you'd change, the one habit you could break. Write it down here:

Your words are your wand.

Ever known anyone to use negative talk when pertaining to him or herself and then start to notice the life that follows? I have. If we can't love ourselves, how can we possibly love anyone else?

Since affirmations from others wear off quickly, the affirmations from you speaking aloud to yourself have very different results. When someone else gives you words of encouragement such as, "You're doing great job; keep up the good work!" or "You're looking great. I love your XYZ," the happy feeling is there and it is nice, but as we know from the "Be your own best friend" story, the feeling wears off quickly. And we can become needy for outside affirmations if we don't take good care of it ourselves. I loved how the authors in How to Be Your Own Best Friend, refer to it as "the glow". It reminds me that when I get attention from people whom I want it from, I do feel a glow that makes me really happy, which is different from any other happy I have felt from myself. I'm a little embarrassed to say this, but when a man I like gives me attention that hits all my love languages, I get this glow, like I was just lifted off of the ground. Then when the man is gone, so is the glow. I'm sure we can all say we've felt it before.

We do have the power to make our own selves feel that kind of love and it's all in your words to yourself. Another quote from How to Be Your Own Best Friend that stuck with me is that in the Bible, Jesus said, "Love thy neighbor as thyself," not better than and not instead of yourself. Loving ourselves by telling ourselves positive things and hearing these words come from our own voices is a gift from our creator. This is my gift to you, if you didn't already know.

You can thank me later. I see it as one of the most important things you can do besides meditation, but we can get into that later.

My Miracle Morning Affirmations

I started my daily affirmations after reading the first two chapters of The Miracle Morning. Hal's story of what brought him to the point of rock bottom hit my gut like a ton of bricks. I got scared. I thought, I'm not going to wait to almost die to start loving my life and myself. I don't want to almost die or even worse, die. Besides, Hal wrote the book so other people didn't have to wait until something tragic happened to make the necessary changes. I had the opportunity to live and the opportunity to make my life into anything I wanted it to be no matter what. No one was going to do it for me. Prior to this, my fucked-up mindset was that everyone else was the answer to my life and someone else was going to do "it" for me. I realized "it" was bring me success, bring me happiness, and bring me the money I needed to support myself right to my doorstep. How many people do you know who think like this? My guess is a lot.

I am here to tell you, that one of the most important thing you can do for yourself and for your future is write down your affirmations to yourself. Even if you don't believe them, you've got to start somewhere and somewhere is always at the bottom. We need fake it 'til we make it. I promise, just like a pathological liar, you will begin to believe your own bullshit. The difference here is that instead of bullshitting other people to make yourself feel good, you are doing it to yourself to fill yourself with your own dreams. You are the greatest XYZ on earth and no one can compare to you. The more you say this, the more it will become engrained into your subconscious mind and you will believe it, I promise. Be lofty with your affirmations; go superhero on yourself.

If we all went through life waiting for other people to praise our accomplishments, we wouldn't make it too far. This is one of my favorite lessons in life so far. Learning to affirm myself would allow me to not look for anyone else to complete me. With plenty of daily personal affirmations, I am far more confident and less likely to need and be at the mercy of finding someone to put me on a pedestal, because I'm already on one. Of course, it's great to hear kind words from others, but when you hear them from yourself, you're on your own personal pedestal and you can paint it any color you want. Soon your affirmations will become a part of you. Say them aloud always. You will begin to become sensitive to other people's words around you. You will start to be choosey to those you put into your immediate circle.

When you fill yourself with love and prayers every morning, these good feelings will continue to build inside you the whole day. It's like doing squats: the second you stop, everything starts to drop. We need consistency and frequency of repetition especially in order to beat back our environmental programming. Our bodies and brains crave consistency, so when we give them that, before we know it, we are designing new dreams and new lives. Improve your affirmations and you will live your best life by your own design. I want you to be really great at lifting yourself up so you won't need others to satisfy your craving.

What are your best three affirmations to yourself?

1)

2)

3)

Rinse and repeat in the mirror.

Use your scenes of sound to trigger you happy

My grandmother would listen to old instrumental music from the 1940s on the radio and whistle while she was cooking. She was as happy as a clam all day every day. She would even whistle to the music while cleaning the house. Every day like clockwork, whistling Dixie, she was! Again, the sound coming from her mouth and back into her own ears was gratifying and affirming her happy while it seasoned every cell in her body.

I will often listen to 1920s through 1940s swing and jazz music while I cook just as she did, so I can keep her spirit alive. I know she's enjoying the music with me. Since her passing, I have become more disciplined in my life, like she was. She was very regimented and everything was in balance and on schedule right down to the music while cooking and cleaning. It was like she was gaining more love and joy to add into each meal and each part of her home, blessing it every step of the way.

She would sit outside and talk to the birds in the yard and she made the cutest birdy sounds you'd ever hear coming from a little old lady. Thinking about it makes me wish I had a recording. She talked to the birds for years—now that's a person who is happy! If you still have your grandparents around, video and audio record them, if you can; you will come to treasure them even more when they are gone.

What are your five favorite songs that are sure to help you feel happy?

1)

2)

3)

4)

5)

To take this further, is there someone's voice in particular that soothes you, someone you would like to listen to daily? Even further, maybe someone you love that you have in your life right now? Or someone that is no longer with us?

If you have a loved one you miss, try to find an old video or some source of sounds from them to add to your list. It may make you a little sad, but the gift here is the person and the remembrance of how special he or she was and how hearing this person's voice brings you joy. If you do or don't have any recordings that is okay; you can start by collecting new ones now. Think of your top three favorite people in the world and record and save awesome clips of them saying things that make you happy and have them stored into your Happy By Design Playlist.

People who make you happy

1)

2)

3)

Try to think of someone you love and get them to voice record saying something nice to you. You can give them some ideas or even write a script. This is going to be fun. Ask your husband or wife to read a script that you have written so you can hear them say the words that would be music to your ear from their lips and save it on your phone so you can play it all the time or when you need a little positive push. I did this exercise with my father because one day I won't be able to call him and hear his voice. It's a grand idea to start gathering memories and you can also return the favor.

Twinkle Toes

My favorite person is my father. I don't get to see him every day as we live in different states; however, I can call him and hear his voice whenever I like.

I remembered something from my childhood that always started my day off happy. My father had a memorable way of waking me up in the mornings. He called me Twinkle Toes, and said, "Wakie, wakie, twinkle toes, time to get up." And he would sing this while tickling my toes at the same time. It was fun and energizing, and it made me laugh first thing in the morning. The last time I saw my father, I asked him if he would be interested in helping his firstborn with a voice clip. Naturally, he agreed. So now I wake myself up with my father's voice, singing twinkle toes. "Wakie, wakie. This is dad. I love you, honey. Twinkle Toes time to get up!" It's one of my favorite affirmations to listen to besides music. I periodically use it. The next time I see my father I'm going to record him telling me a story like he did when I was a child, and I will keep it for a rainy day. I highly suggest you start voice recording your loved ones. Sing songs together, poke fun, and hit record; it will be one of your greatest possessions.

Your list of sounds is yours to design is any way you like. Choose things that make you feel inspired, encouraged, and most of all, happy and well. I encourage you to update your list and keep it fresh; after all, we can always use happiness in our lives. I am going to do this as something special with all of my favorite people.

And one last point before we leave our sense of sound. Ever hear that men and women hear things differently?

A study at the University of Sheffield and published in the journal NeuroImage found differences in the way the male and female brains process voice sounds. Females typically process voice sounds in Wernicke's area in the left cerebral hemisphere. Males tend to process male voice sounds in Wernicke's area, but process female voice sounds in the auditory portion of the right hemisphere used for processing melody lines.

Men:

- Tend to have less acute hearing overall
- Their hearing differences become more pronounced throughout life

The things men hear that make them happy:

The Harley motor of the motorcycle when it starts up or the sound of a fast car with a big engine really gets them going. Tattoo guns, fire arms, wrestling matches, sporting events or any type of race makes men feel power from these things. The sound of women having orgasms, again, is music to their ears. Hearing the dog bark, the sound of power tools, lawn mowers, you know the "Tim the Tool-Man Taylor" type of stuff, and then they love to hear themselves grunt and growl like animals.

As a man, sounds I love to hear include:

1)

2)

3)

Women, on the other hand, are much different. They tend to have more acute hearing overall and are easily distracted by sound.

As early as age eleven, females tend to be distracted by noise levels that are about 10 times softer than the levels that comparable boys find distracting.

Females tend to hear better than males (have less acute hearing), and this difference only becomes more pronounced throughout life. As compared to a male voice, the female voice is more difficult for males to listen to (Funny, explains why with the majority of men, I feel like I am never heard.) To increase the likelihood of being heard by a male, females need to lower their voice pitch and keep it even (avoid pitch variation), speak louder, and lower inflections at the end of sentences.

Other Sounds We Women Love

We love the sound of the cash register ringing when we are out getting some retail therapy. The sound of text message notifications, the hair salon gossip, or our significant other telling us how much he or she loves us can be music to our ears. We feel calm from the soft sounds of music while having a facial or massage. The sound of our breath in yoga class, the sound of birds chirping, the sounds of the ocean can have us feeling very tranquil and calm. Waterfalls, ocean waves at the beach, anything coastal, the wind, birds, and sounds from the rainforest are all sounds that create feelings within us.

One of my favorite things to hear that just puts me into sedation is a fireplace fire crackling. Not only does it make me warm, but also the look and sound of it, soothes me.

Your pets making noises, such as cats meowing or dogs barking, growling, and being playful, are all sounds we love.

As a woman, sounds I love to hear include:

1)

2)

3)

All of these things bring us power and that's why you should take note of what that is for you and make note of it so you can keep adding to your personal power.

If you like comedy, listen to comedy more and laugh, this programs your cells and burns calories, too. Research conducted by Vanderbilt University Medical Center revealed that laughing burns calories by causing your heart rate to rise by 10 to 20 percent. As your heart rate rises, your metabolism increases as well, which means you'll continue to burn calories once you stop laughing.

Some people are taken by listening to poetry; if that's you, why not have your significant other recite and record poetry from your favorite poet so you can listen to it always. Or better yet, is there anyone's voice or a certain tone of voice you love to hear? I happen to love that deep southern drawl in country western singers like George Straight. Why not find someone who has that voice that just turns you on and record them saying something that is music to your ears? It's this type of outside of the box thinking that keeps us stimulated and living happy lives.

What about the sounds of being silent? Is it really quiet?

I often find it much more enjoyable to listen to nothing. Silence at home, silence while driving and just enough to hear nothing.

What sounds make you happy?

Sounds You Want to Remove	**Sounds You Want to Add**
1	
2	
3	

Sense of Touch

The ability to touch and feel is the most powerful sense of all. Skin has the highest number of neurons or nerve cells, which gives us the ability to perceive many different sensations. Through our skin we can feel relaxation, vulnerability, comfort, temperature, texture, fear, joy, and frequency, a sensory trigger that has the most power.

Since physical touch is one of my love languages (see the work of Gary Chapman for more on this topic), this subject happens to invigorate me a pinch more than the rest. I am one of those people who love to be touched. Hugs, kisses, and hand holding makes me feel wanted, comforted, and most of all, connected.

But some many things go into our senses of touch or can touch us. For example, the weather.

Temperature

The temperature of the weather that touches our skin can bring us joy. Have you ever known anyone to be a warm weather person or someone who loves the freezing cold? This has to be one of the easiest no brainers when it comes to things we can change to increase our happiness. The temperature touches us on a daily basis and can either comfort our daily lives or make us very uncomfortable.

I know that with my warm weather personality, I am definitely more irritable or easily saddened by little things when its gloomy or cold out. On a nice warm weather day, not a lot can get me down in the dumps when I am enjoying the beach weather. Plain and simple, if you are a warm weather person, live in it. If you are a cold weather advocate, gravitate towards it. There is no sense in expecting to be happy and living life to your fullest if you are not living within your temperature personality.

Sense of physical touch

For as long as I can remember, I have loved physical touch. My grandmother would have a very warm, inviting, genuine hug when we arrived to visit. I was her little angel. We would hug all the time. Sometimes we would just stop what we were doing and hug. It brings a tear to my eyes just thinking about how much she loved me and the warmth she held for me and I for her. We would hold hands when we went for walks and play bread and butter when walking through a post, we would hold our hands up and walk on either side of the post and sing, "bread and butter! Peanut butter and jelly, salt and pepper." Oh, those were the days! Those days very much shaped my happy. I'm sure you have some special memories like this that you can remember bringing you joy. When we connect through touch, our energy is healing given the feature points to oxytocin, which is described as "the bonding hormone." The simple truth of the matter is if you want a healthy mind-body and a healthy relationship, you should probably ramp up the physical contact.

Even if you are not in a romantic relationship, being in contact with the ones close to you is highly healthy; touch is shaping up to be the ultimate mind-body medicine. "Lack of touch seriously impacts one's life," according to developmental psychologist and nonverbal communication expert Matthew J. Hertenstein, Ph.D., of DePauw University. Michael Richardson writes, "This hormone and neurotransmitter, once thought to be crucial only for babies and mothers, is now believed to be a super hormone that helps with everything from illness recovery, life length, addiction recovery, depression recovery and anxiety prevention. This hormone lays the biological foundation and structure for connecting to others." So, if you enjoy hand holding or hugging, make the connection more with the people you love. If you're not a touchy-feely kind of person, you might like petting an animal; they are live energy, too.

Heartbeats and Hugs

The best thing about hugs are not only releasing the bonding hormones but the heartbeat.

The emotion of joy when feeling someone else's heart beat can elevate our mood just through our awareness that we are alive and alive together. When we hug, the trickle-down effects of feeling good throughout the body causes a decrease in heart rate and a drop in the stress hormones cortisol and norepinephrine. After all, we developed next to our mother's heart for nine months prior to birth, listening to it beat and feeling its vibrations. Our heartbeat is what keeps us alive, and it's cool that we can feel the other person's heartbeat through a hug, a good hug.

This reminds me of a story I once read by Emily Crane for the Daily Mail Australia about twin baby Jaime Ogg having complications at birth. Mother Kate Ogg, delivered two twin premature baby boys two minutes apart, and one baby, Jaime, was too weak and stopped breathing. His mother asked to hold the lifeless infant, and his father, David Ogg, removed his shirt and hopped into the hospital bed to hold their baby Jamie between them for once last tender embrace. What happened next was nothing short of a miracle. While Kate and David Ogg held their baby in between their two warm bodies and their two beating hearts, this act of love for the child miraculously brought their baby back to life.

A Hug a Day Will Keep the Doctor Away

According to Stacey Colino of Health Online, people who perceived greater social support were less likely to come down with a cold, and the researchers calculated that the stress-buffering effects of hugging explained 32 percent of that beneficial effect.

The more physical affection you receive, the happier and healthier you will be. Your body needs hugs and other forms of touch, just like it needs food and water, so make an effort to get more hugs daily. "Hugging protects people who are under stress from the increased risk for colds usually associated with stress," Colino writes.

Let's secure more hugs in our lives simply by making an effort to be more affectionate with family members and friends. Remember, giving hugs is as beneficial as receiving them, so make a point to initiate hugs often with your partner and other loved ones. If you need to throw yourself into it with a 5,4,3,2,1 challenge (if you're not a physical touch person) then, close your eyes and put your sense of sight to rest and enjoy solely what the sense of touch has to offer. I'd be willing to bet your other senses will heighten during this experiment. My challenge to you is to hug one person per day for the next 30 days. Give it the 30 days to create a habit. What a great habit to take up, too.

If you are nervous about a hug, you can be courteous about it, and say something like, "I could use a hug", "I'm a hugger" or "Can I give you a hug?" There are areas in the world where people are more connected and experience the sense of love. Sadly, but not surprisingly, having little money equates to more of love on a global level. In 2006 and 2007, The Gallup Organization asked people in 136 countries whether they had experienced love the previous day.

People in Rwanda and the Philippines received the highest love ratios of more than 90 percent, researchers found on a typical day. The United States ranked 81 percent.

This reminds me of a sign I found in a second-hand store and had for years, it reads, "No one is poor with love to spend." When I saw this inspirational piece of stained glass, it melted my heart. I enjoy decorating my personal space priceless reminders like this so I never lose track of what's really important. Love is the stuff of the universe. Allowing yourself to receive love is loving yourself and loving yourself changes the world one hug at a time.

Physical Touch and Social Interaction

I always love to ask a lot of questions while doing hair to better educate myself about my clients, what they do, who, they are and mostly what makes them happy. I have a client who is a psychotherapist. Since she too sees multiple people each day, I asked "What do you think the majority of your patients would benefit from to make them happier?" Her answer was not surprising, "more social interaction."

It's like plant roots not being connected into the soil and the ground. When you pull a plant from the ground, it dies. We need to be around each other for our mental health, to hug (feel hearts beating), connect our energies, make eye contact, and all kinds of contact to feel more alive and well. The next time you're around someone you are close to, just pull in for a connective hug. Some have grown to feel uncomfortable with touching others for various reasons; however, out of our comfort zone is where the miracle happens. Just do it.

Human Touch – Sex and Physical Togetherness

We are all connected to each other and connected to the Earth. Love is good for us, kissing is good for us, and massages are all good for us, and sex is really good for us. In my experience, during sexual contact, we exchange energy so I love to be picky about with whom I exchange energy. My energy is precious and I want to be sure that person is worthy of my energy and I of his. It's another way for me to be selfish. I wouldn't want to upload someone's energy that I do not admire or want wholeheartedly connected to my mind-body.

Through research and personal experience, I've learned about the energy that can be exchanged between two people. Body heat through skin contact is a great feeling and makes us more one with the other person by way of hormones, connection, and of course body fluids.

We must understand that the person we choose to have sexual encounters with will have an effect on our personal energy field (aura). The person that we engage with intimately becomes entwined with our own personal energy field and their aura meshes with ours. The combination can either bring negativity into your life or a positive flow. I have experienced this first hand, so take it from me, this is a thing. Never sleep with someone you wouldn't want to be energetically connected with. Just think of a person you might know who sleeps with multiple partners and considers sex to be a meaningless act, maybe that person is you or has been you. Your aura could become confused and more so, broken, by left behind conflicting spiritual debris. Bad habits are hard to break, but awareness is easy.

With positive interactions and physical connection, we can stimulate a healthier body and life.

Psychologist Tiffany Field, director of the Touch Research Institute at the University of Miami School of Medicine says, when you're hugging or cuddling with someone, [he or she is] stimulating pressure receptors under your skin in a way that leads to a cascade of events including an increase in vagal activity." The Vagus nerve is the longest cranial nerve in your body. By increasing your vagal tone, this activates the parasympathetic nervous system, and having a higher vagal tone means that your body can relax faster after stress.

One theory is that stimulation of the vagus nerve triggers an increase in oxytocin levels. One of the best ways using your sense of touch would be have more physical contact which causes a decrease in heart rate and a drop in the stress hormones cortisol and norepinephrine. A 2010 study from Ohio State University found that couples with more positive communication heal faster from wounds.

Human Touch-Have A Massage or a Facial

Human touch is thought to improve mood in ways similar to exercise. I go twice each week to Happy Feet where they soak my feet in tea and give me a full head to toe massage for one hour for about $30. Being happy and healthy surely starts with me and spreads onto life around me. Taking care of myself with frequent massages has a magnificent effect on my level of happiness.

Other things that I love beside regular body massages are going for facials. I think that a facial massage is actually more relaxing than a body massage. Having my face exfoliated, steamed, and massaged with a focus on pressure points helps activate my lymphatic system and give me the feeling that I'm doing something nice for myself with great glowing results. One of the reasons facials give a great glow is not only because of the exfoliation but also because the lymph is being stimulated during the lymphatic massage. The human body accumulates all sorts of waste and toxins that it must remove to stay healthy. The lymphatic system is the network of various organs, tissues, and vessels that help keep the body clean beneath the skin's surface. I treat myself to the things I enjoy and help make me a healthier person and I hope you do, too. Through massage, we can relieve our fight or flight signals and stop the cortisol production, which will put you into a fat burning mode, a win-win.

Body Brushing

I see so many benefits from my morning ritual of body brushing. Not only am I stimulating my sense of touch, but I am actually waking myself up by getting my lymphatic system moving. Body brushing is one of four known ways to stimulate your lymphatic system to get it working better. Many lymph nodes are found just below the surface of the skin. Many massage spas offer lymphatic massages, but even gentle skin brushing or rubbing of nodes like the ones below your jaw will go a long way. Since tactile nerves lay right underneath the skin, body brushing can calm the brain, lower stress hormones, and help regulate cortisol. This, in turn, can help us sleep better, lose weight more easily, have more energy and more.

As you brush your skin, blood circulation to that area is increased, and increased circulation enhances the flow of lymph fluid through the skin. Brushing improves the drainage of lymph in the skin, helping remove damaging toxins. A poor lymph flow is the reason for many health complaints like a poor immunity and fluid retention.

In fact, this practice has been exercised for thousands of years, from the ancient Greeks, to the Japanese, and the American Indians, where they used dry corncobs to brush off dead cells of the skin from their bodies.

I've also read on detoxbodycleanse.com that body brushing is another way to cleanse your kidney and liver through by stimulating your lymph. I've even heard that if you do it every day, in two months the color of your eyes will be lighter and this is a clear indication that your liver has become clean.

Other benefits include, by helping the skin get rid of toxins, you are actually reducing the load off your liver and kidneys. When you dry brush, and as you remove your skin's dead cells, you are then making room for new and fresh skin cells to grow. In general, dry brushing helps improve your body get rid of waste and toxins, increase blood circulation, helps slow down skin aging, and even alleviates muscular tension and fluid retention. It is a powerful yet simple therapy that can impact the body positively.

Taking a few small steps to invest in yourself for better healthier happier life will make all the difference.

Earth's Energizing Healing Elements

I remember as a child running around on a warm sunny day playing on the grass in the front yard barefoot and running through the sprinklers with my brothers. Little did anyone really know that this was a healthy thing to do and would aid to a healthy longer life instantly with contact.

The connection with the ground has been proven to elevate mood, energize the body, and bring healing to us.

Connection with the Earth – Grounding or Earthing

I'm not sure if any of my readers have ever heard of this before, but you can learn the basics on www.earthing.com. Did you ever wonder why your indoor plants aren't quite as healthy as the ones outside? Or have you ever wondered why you yourself feel better being outside? It's all the elements our planet gives us to live the way we were intended to.

When I first learned about grounding and energy, it was from my middle brother, Tommy. My brother is paralyzed at the moment but he will walk and run again one day soon. When that day comes, we will be racing each other on the beach barefoot soaking up the earth's energy and loving it. Tommy is continuously researching ways to resource energy to heal his body and walk again. When he finds research, he will do cool things like buy the book or the video tape and mail it to one family member to watch/read and we keep the ball rolling. Tommy and I both have a love for sharing the latest findings in the world of health with our friends and family. We truly want others to be as healthy and happy as they can and we can all have fun working on it together.

The grounding video from www.earthing.com explains how the Earth has an abundant supply of electrons for us to upload through our body, which I will explain more in this section. But for now, I wanted to talk about how I can actually feel the energy coming in through my feet when I walk on the grass barefoot. Also, when touching a tree, I can feel the electrons or energy coming into the palm of my hand and up my arm. I have to say it makes me feel good. It feels like a tingling sensation of what I would describe as a slight vibration or frequency. I may be a higher vibration type of person so I am able to feel energy more than most people. From what I have learned from earthing.com and many medical studies is that since our body is mostly water and minerals, this makes us great conductors of energy. The free electrons on the surface of the Earth are easily transferred to the human body as long as there is direct contact. I have also read that we are depleted banks of electricity due to the fact that we wear synthetically-soled shoes which, act as insulators; so, even when we are outside, we do not connect with the Earth's electric field.

Also, when we are in homes and office buildings, we are also insulated and unable to receive the Earth's balancing energies. James Oschman, Ph.D., an internationally-renowned expert on energy medicine, describes the phenomenon thusly: "One of my colleagues came in from the West Coast. She had a bad case of jet lag. I told her to take her shoes and socks off and step outside on the grass for 15 minutes. When she came back in, she was completely transformed. Her jet lag was gone. That is how fast Earthing works. Anyone can try this. If you don't feel well, for whatever reason, just make barefoot contact with the Earth for a few minutes and see what happens."

So many studies prove grounding increases the surface charge on the red blood cells, thereby reducing viscosity and clumping. In 2013, a group of doctors, including Gaetan Chevalier, Stephen T. Sinatra, James L. Oschman, and Richard M. Delany, ran a series of highly organized medical tests on ten healthy human subjects. The researchers found through testing their blood samples before and after two hours of surface contact with the earth that grounding appears to be one of the simplest and yet most profound interventions for helping reduce cardiovascular risk and cardiovascular events.

Consequently, grounding leads to rapid equalization of the electrical potential of the body with the potential of the Earth through an almost instantaneous transfer of electrons from soil to the body. This has been the natural bioelectrical environment of the human body and of other organisms throughout most of evolutionary history.

There has been an insurmountable amount of coverage on the subject through medical testing, publications, on YouTube channels, and television documentaries in regards to the instant health benefits of being in contact with the Earth's surface.

After thorough research, I'm convinced that we are one with our Earth and the benefits are endless.

The best form of grounding comes from the Ocean

I'd love to talk a few minutes about this because I know the sand at the beach to actually be a conductor of energy that fills our banks with yet another healthy component, electrons. Even when we walk on the sand, the dirt, the grass with our bare feet, we are able to upload electrons from the Earth, which fill our body with an energy and health that is necessary in life.

Why? Because our connection to the Earth and ground is electrified by the Earth's core; sand has metal energy conducting elements in it. At the beach the little bits of gold in the sand carry and conduct the energy from the Earth's core and, as a double whammy, the water is another huge conductor of energy. This is the best way to get the Earth's minerals and energy through conductive materials. Studies show that being in the ocean or at the beach for 20 minutes per day is the best way to ground and upload the electrons our bodies need to be at our healthiest. Doctors were prescribing trips to the shore or visits to "bathing hospitals" — special clinics that offered seawater bath treatments — as early as the 18th century. But only recently have scientists begun studying the ocean's health benefits experimentally. Research shows that spending time by the ocean has many positive effects on health and well-being, says epidemiologist Lora Fleming of the University of Exeter in England.

We might as well call our oceans the fountain of youth. Breathing the fresh, salt air does wonders for the respiratory system, and those with asthma, bronchitis, sinus pressure, and coughing will notice a difference in their conditions after just one day at the beach. Inhaling a sea mist filled with negatively charged ions, or molecules that attach to your lungs also boosts your immune system, according to naturopathic doctor Connie Hernandez. In addition, proponents claim that swimming in seawater opens pores in the skin to allow the absorption of sea minerals and the expulsion of disease-causing toxins from the body. Magnesium-rich seawater can also relax your muscles, reduce stress, and help induce sleep.

Any chance I get, I walk on the ground barefoot. I often drink my coffee or have breakfast in the backyard while grounding with me feet on the grass. It's a lovely feeling to touch my bare skin to the grass and dirt. If anyone likes to garden, I say do it barefoot and get even more therapeutic results.

Animals Make People Happy

Studies have shown that people who live with pets are happier people since they receive a lot of love from their animals. Dr. Alan M. Beck, director of the Center for the Human-Animal Bond at the Purdue University College of Veterinary Medicine says, "Pets lower stress by fulfilling our need for touch," which I find comforting. And what's more, they feel the same way about it. If you're grooming a horse, not only will you experience the relaxation response, Beck says, but put your hand on the horse, and you'll feel its heart rate slow down. Same when you pet your dog: "There's a certain excitement at first, but then its heart rate goes down." Just being around an animal decreases your blood pressure, which is one physical measure of stress. Ever since work by Dr. Beck and colleagues first showed that petting a dog or cat lowers a person's blood pressure, this has been found to be true with other animals as well.

If you are struggling with loneliness and feel like there's a piece of the puzzle missing, be around animals, or volunteer at the fish store, the animal shelter, or a cat society. Do something to fill your tank with the free joys that come from petting an animal; after all, it's going to make you healthy and happy. Ever wonder why animals are used in therapy in the hospitals to trigger some happy into cancer patients, the elderly, and the children? Because the feel of a dog's fur and feeling its love can actually overpower what ails us. Running your fingers through fur will elevate your mood within an instant.

If you are going through a break up, lost someone to death, or just need some unconditional love get an animal to love and who will love you. Dr. Alan also confirms that people with pets are less likely to say they feel loneliness, which is one common source of stress. This is both because animals provide companionship and because they encourage friendly interactions with other people.

If you don't care for animals there are always physical possessions that will definitely pique your interest.

Physical Possessions Can Trigger You Happy

I had a 2005 Nissan Maxima for 13 years, a car that could be called a sleeper or a family sedan, but it had a rocket engine. When you saw it coming, you'd think it was filled with a mother, a father, children, and probably a small doggy. But no, I gunned down the street like a battleship and the vehicle looked like it was going slow just from the shape. It didn't stick out like a race car because it's silver (most common color on the road) so it blends in well. On top of these key points, it was super comfortable. I would get into it and almost bounce because of how cushy the seats were, and it was like sitting on a couch in your own living room if you were perched on the back seat. The car was perfect for long trips and it had plenty of trunk space.

When I originally purchased this vehicle, I saw the brand-new model on the showroom floor. I circled it in pure amazement of how hot I would look in this prize. It was conventional, with a racing flare, exactly what I needed and wanted. I sat in its beauty and the felt the seats hugging my body and I knew it was for me. Of course, the one in the showroom was brand new and I went home that night thinking, the car would be amazing, but seriously? It was a lot of money and I wasn't making that kind of money at the time. So, I looked online for the same model but a few years older. I found one about a half-hour drive away with approximately 15,000 miles on it for like $20,000 instead of the $35,000-$40,000 the dealer wanted. The car looked identical, and they had put in tint all the way around because they had a baby who traveled in the back seat. Everyone at home tried to poop on my dream of having this car, but I knew what made me feel great, and I decided I was worth it.

At the time I had finished cosmetology school and I was now a hairdresser making my way in the world. I felt like the car was going to help me seal the deal with myself every damn day. We need tokens and prizes that we give ourselves to show our achievement and growth. Sometimes a new car can help your growth by making you extra happy every time you see it, feel it, touch the steering wheel, sit in the seat, and feel it hug you the way you need it to, to make you feel the joy and allow you to step up your game and upgrade your life. There's something to be said about your image and image may have something to do with the vehicle you select to get you from point A to point B. Just like Batman and his Batmobile. The Batmobile was exactly what Bruce Wayne needed to be Batman. Don't you think that badass armored vet gave Batman the energy he needed? Hell, yes, it did! I'm sure Vicki Vale thought it was pretty sexy and made him that much more mysterious.

Buy Clothes You Love to Touch or Feel Against Your Skin

High-end, quality clothing makes me feel really good. When I put something on that is made well, which could mean is it is tailored and it hugs me in the right places, I feel more confident and happier. Stuff like that shouldn't be overlooked. Clothing is with us all day when it's on us. It's touching our bodies, so make sure what you wear suits you, pleases you, and brings you joy. Treat yourself, don't cheat yourself. When you cover your body, remember always go better than normal, as you can never be too well dressed. People really notice when you take pride in your attire. You are a gift, so wrap yourself like one. Dress as though it's the best day of your life. Remember you are the gift that keeps on giving so do yourself lots of favors and it will pay off.

For example, I'm in the store looking for a shirt for a party that evening, when all of the sudden I notice four rows down a dress hanging on the end as if someone had it and put it back. Right away, I knew it was a dress perfect for me. Anxiously, I walked over to it, hoping someone wasn't going to see it before I got there. I picked it up and confirmed the cut, the color, the trim were awesome. I knew it would fit, but I always try something on first. Sure enough, after trying, it's me to the T.

Clothing touches all of our bodies on a daily basis, but does it feel good? Have you ever noticed the difference between the feelings you get from different fabrics? The different weight and thread counts, does one make you feel better than the other? For instance, I happen to feel really cool when I'm wearing a fur coat because it feels so soft and good and it reminds me of an animal I'd like to pet and it becomes interactive also when wearing something of that nature people want to pet me while wearing it such things. I think it's fun! Any way to be more connected and social is a good thing.

I'm growing to notice the difference between well-made clothing and clothing that does nothing for my body. You know me I like things that do me favors. The difference between an article of clothing an outfit that makes you feel like a million bucks? I like to spend my time with things like that because you know what life is the quality of what we make it. So, the next time you're out looking for something to clothe your body, remember to dress as though you're a gift, a gift to yourself and a gift to the world. Don't dress for the job you have, dress for the one you want. Dress as if it's the best day of your life, because it is. Opportunity comes to those who welcome it and are dressed for it.

Every morning you wake up and decide what you're going to put on your body so make sure it brings you joy and makes you feel like the rock star that you are. I tend to love my stylish faux leather pants; they have become my signature go-to. When I touch them, they make me feel great and when I'm wearing them, they make other people smile. So why not? When you find your signature favorite clothing, treat yourself; it's an investment and advertisement for yourself to feel and show your value for what you love. In my mind, you can't put a dollar amount on investing in yourself because it's all for a great cause because you are the gift that keeps on giving.

Personal Space & Home Comfort What brings you comfort?

Bedding

A place where we spend the majority of our time is sleeping in our bed. Having a quality bed will make us want to snuggle in have great dreams. Your bed holds you all night so you are well rested and wake up feeling like a million bucks. I have heard so many people complain about their beds. If you are having trouble finding the perfect level comfort be a little more creative. I began my bed journey long ago and bought all of this memory foam. But the thing with memory foam is if you don't rotate it and put a reminder in your phone, you are bound to have that body indention. After going through a ton of different types of beds I got smart and bought a memory foam mattress without the springs or anything in it. I flipped the memory foam part over to the really solid bottom part that is hard like a firm mattress and I added a 1.5-inch foam topper with a pillow top mattress pad, so I have the firmness that I like with a hint of cushion. I've had this bed longer than most others and I think I may have myself a winner. Get creative if you haven't found the right combination that works for you.

A quality bed, soft blankets, or satin sheets are treats you deserve. After all, if we don't sleep well, we aren't well. Our bodies need to rejuvenate and rest and doing so on a comfortable level that brings us joy is something that we definitely have control over. Touch your sheets. How do they feel? Take a trip down to the bedding section at a local store and climb into some of those beds on the showroom floor. Feel the sheets, speak with the sales representatives, and have them take you through some different materials and thread counts. I have a best friend Wendy, who wouldn't go a night without her 1,000-thread-count sheets.

How Does Your Flooring Feel?

One of my absolute favorite things to feel is a nice faux fur rug sitting right in front of the fireplace on a cold winter night. What a treat. Picture this, you walk into your house after a long day, you sit and remove your shoes and walk across the soft rug and feel the fibers with a soft pillow like material beneath your feet. Isn't that a small pleasure after along hard day? I like to sit on the couch and run my feet over the top of the soft furry rug, as this makes me feel so relaxed and grateful. Spend a few minutes enjoying your rug if you have one or get one if you like them. Even if you've never given it a thought, give it one now as an awareness to your sense of touch. Do you love your floors? If not, its time to find the ones you do. Could you imagine if you loved everything from your ground up and everything sparked joy?

Some people prefer hardwood floors, tile, slate or rock type materials that bring them joy. It's time to explore what you love to feel around you.

Bath

The joy of having nice soft fluffy towels is one of those things I can control and on which I love to splurge. Treat yourself to a new fluffy towel set, a cushy memory foam bath rug, or maybe a new bathrobe. Many of the things we use in the bathroom touch our bodies on a daily basis. There's a lot of bargains to be had out there and we can do a pretty good job at keeping nice things in place for ourselves by shopping wisely if money is tight. Go through your bath towels and sift through to find the ones that don't bring you joy and replace them with something new that you love. Your body is a gift and it should be held and touched by only the things that make you feel lovely. Our sense of touch is connecting to all of the rest, so let's take notes to upgrade you and your surroundings because you are worth it.

Take a trip down to TJ Max Home Goods, Macy Bath Essentials, or Bed Bath and Beyond when you are ready to explore. When you get to the bath section, take a walk through and feel the towels one brand at a time. When you feel your way through each one, you will allow your sense of touch come alive. To get a clear indication of what feels good to you, try closing your eyes when you feel each towel. With your eyes closed, sense the way you feel and imagine where you might be when using such a towel. When you find the one that is like no other, caress the towel, swing the towel around your body, tie it around your waist, pat your face with it—how does it make you feel? If the answer is like a million bucks, then I would take it because it will add value to you and your life. Upgrade your selection of linens that will touch your precious body because you are worth it. Now you can enjoy your new towels that tickle your sense of touch every day.

How to decide what items you touch that bring you Joy

Deciding what items bring you joy is a very personal experience. I follow Marie Kondo, the guru of organization. She preaches the Konmari Japanese art of decluttering and organizing. If you follow her way, you will do it once and never have to declutter again. Marie teaches a way to identify which items bring you joy so you can rid your personal space of the excess noise that holds us back. By holding us back I mean, things that distract us, crowd us, or weigh on our physical lives like a weighted backpack that we often don't know is there until it's gone. Marie teaches her followers how to identify things that bring you joy so you may use this method in all areas of your life,

Everything that is a possession is treated as a prize and is valued and thanked for the purpose it serves. Clothing is folded like flag and is stood upright instead of flattened and piled like junk. We stack the abundance and showcase our trophies. To take it a little further, colors start light and move into dark; it's a Feng Shui art to give you the feeling of organization and structure. You will notice the difference, I promise. I respect her art in so many ways because she's right: if you can learn that internal feeling of what makes you feel like a gift when you physically touch it, you can use it to ignite everything in your life.

In Marie's decluttering exercise, you go through everything you own by category, not by room, and you physically touch each item. For example, your shirts, have them in a pile in front of you; this is a spiritual activity for you to see how you feel about each item.

When I did this, there were shirts that I would never get rid of in a million years, Shirts that made me look and feel like I was a better person. Tops that would make me feel so good when I put them on and even saw them hanging, I would feel like royalty at the mere sight of them. Blouses that, if my home was on fire, I would lead the search and rescue team to save my precious blouse as if it were my child! You get my point. Others, I would wait out the possibilities, options, and weigh the pros and cons, if you will. I learned quickly that the second I began to evaluate any said item, I realized it wasn't a prize to me and it was dispensable. There was my answer right there. It's the point of absolute certainty where your brain says, "hell yes" without another thought to follow. The second you start to think and ponder the choice then it's a "no." Could you imagine if every aspect of your life was brilliant? It can be and it will be.

The impressive part of the Konmari art is when you are discarding something; you thank it for its service in your life. For me, this has been a life-changing experience.

What 3 things triggers you happy that you can feel?

1

2

3

What would you like to upgrade?

What you want to remove   **What you'd love to add**

1
2
3

How will this enrich my life?

HAPPY and you KNOW it

For my last piece of paradise, I will leave you with a few key components of what I believe are the heart of a healthy lifestyle. Everyone's body is different so please, do what feels good to you. This is your time to explore what gives you the ultimate essence of healing and absolute bliss in your life. When you get to know your body and what it needs, it is sure to lead you in a direction of knowledge and strength.

Sunlight, Oxygen, Nutrients, Water, Exercise, and Meditation

Regardless if you are a warm weather personality or a cool weather personality, we all need sunlight to grow and nourish our bodies. We are a product of our earth; therefore, we need many of the same components that plants need to live and live healthy. Much like a plant, we need oxygen, sunlight, nutrients, and hydration to stay alive and be well. We humans are mobile, so we require movement to keep ourselves in tiptop shape with plenty of exercise. As mammals, our brains are continually working to keep the mechanics of our systems functioning, and with function can come fatigue. I always use water to help keep energized especially when I feel sluggish; this usually means I need to hydrate more. Nutrients are equally important to a strong engine, if we want to go fast, we must insert the gas. By gas, I mean fuel, fuel for our tanks. Don't get me wrong; I do love a good ice cream sundae, but 90 percent of the time, it's green, fruits, and grains. Lastly, one of my favorite good habits to practice is meditation. I use meditation to stop my busy life, be still, and allow my brain to process as a way to recover from stress, and we all have stress.

Sunlight and Vitamin D

Spending time in the sunlight and absorbing vitamin D is another way to design a happy life. Spend more time in sunlight to increase your dopamine sensitivity through the production of Vitamin D. Allow the sunlight to touch your skin. The reflection of the sun off of the sand and the ocean is a great way to get your daily dose of vitamin D. As long as you're smothered in SPF, getting some sunshine every day is good for your health. Vitamin D from the sun improves autoimmune protection, increases endorphins, lowers the risk of many kinds of cancer, and enhances bone health. If you cannot get to the ocean every day, like I'm unable to, sit in the sun for 10 minutes per day.

After my shower in the mornings I sit out on the back deck with my coffee and enjoy the morning sunlight. The birds sing, squirrels run around, and the earth is alive. It's nice to enjoy peace by observing the sunlight warming my skin. I often take my shoes off and put my bare feet on the dirt while I'm at it. A little sunlight, connection, and coffee never hurt anybody.

When it's not very sunny out, I enjoy the use of a low powered Vitamin D tanning bed to kiss my skin with the UV lights. Not even five minutes into the bed light and my whole body thanks me with a feeling of relief. I can literally feel the production of Vitamin D being absorbed through my skin. I am instantly healthier and happier.

Exposure to either the sun's or a tanning booth's UV rays helps your body produce vitamin D. Vitamin D itself has been attributed to the prevention of plenty of diseases, including colon cancer, depression, high blood pressure, breast cancer, fibromyalgia, prostate cancer, seasonal affective Disorder (SAD), PMS, arthritis, psoriasis, diabetes, and osteoporosis.

According to 2005 article in USA Today titled "Vitamin D Research May Have Doctors Prescribing Sunshine," vitamin D can actually stifle abnormal cell growth and the formation of blood vessels that feed tumors, which in turn can help to prevent a smattering of cancers. It may be hard to believe that natural or artificial sunlight can help in the prevention of all of these diseases, but it's important to remember one thing: the only way that your body can produce vitamin D is by absorbing UV rays and converting them into this essential vitamin.

I have noticed a common denominator in unhappy people I have come in contact with and it's shocking the high percentage of them are extremely pale. Just a little exposure to UV light will make a huge difference. When interviewing indoor tanning salons simply ask the concrete question "how much UVB, (in % of UVA), does your tanning bed with highest amount of UVB have?" If the answer is above 5% UVB (in North America) or 2.3% (in Europe), you are good. You might find that many salon-operators do not know how much UVB there is in their tanning beds, but that, I believe, is about to change in the future.

If you or anyone you know has a tough time living happily, it's time to bring some sunshine into your life and produce the key Vitamin D. Like I said earlier, without sunlight plants cannot live, they would die. I should know, every year for Christmas my friend Chris bring me a succulent plant and hangs Christmas ornaments on it for me to keep at my workstation. There is no direct or indirect sunlight anywhere near my workspace, therefore, within a few months, Chris receives the sad faced text message with a planter pot with no plant. Think of yourself as the flower: you want to blossom and become long lasting. Hit the tanning bed once or twice per week and take some vitamin D supplements. Periodically I use the liquid stuff I can just put into my water or under my tongue, when I can't get 10 minutes of sunshine. It's easy and it works. I think a lot of people are just like myself and don't like taking pills so the liquid is a good substitute. Find the one you like or simply get some rays on your skin.

Oxygen Anyone?

Feeling the oxygen enter my lungs and being aware of it from time to time is a blessing. I often notice myself taking a deep breath when I get settled into my mediation. Other times I notice my breath when my brain gets overloaded with too many options, decisions, and deadlines. It's like my body knows the benefit of a little more oxygen for clarity and relief. It's time to take a few deep breaths and enjoy the air we are able to breath.

My roommate told me about an Indian man named Sudarshan Kriya who does this certain breathing technique that basically simulates going on a run or high intensity exercise. He took me through the basics one day and it was 30 seconds slow deep breathing, one minute of a little faster, then faster and then really fast like I was on a real run. Just sitting and breathing like that, I was amazed at how energized I became. So, I began to do it as a routine for about five minutes in the morning before meditation just to wake myself up more and I'm so much more alert during the day. The amount of oxygen that had been forced into my brain and body was powerful and I feel stronger doing it. Even though exercise may be a part of your daily routine, this kind of breathing is helpful. For those of you that need a little nudge into exercise action, try this breathing exercise online and some yoga exercises, and how to combine them to help flush oxygen into your lungs and into your brain. It is called Paranoiac Breathing Technique.

It is guaranteed to make you feel and look younger, as it's all about flushing your lungs with oxygen.

Have Some Water with Me

One of my all-time favorite books is by Dr. Fereydoon Batmanghelidj, M.D., Your Body's Many Cries For Water. I've read this book four times and purchased it seven times, as gifts for people. I was at a friend's place when I noticed this book on the coffee table. It has a glass of water on the front, and I was drawn to it. I flipped through all of the diagrams and photos and saw photo what Dr. Batmanghelidj called waterways with food getting clogged in digestive tracks and all kinds of pictures of what we are unknowingly doing to our bodies by not drinking enough water nor taking in sea salt within that water. I highly suggest reading the book. We are mostly water and per Dr. Batmanghelidj water is essential through all phases of the body's growth. Now, if we take water, the pattern of life can go up to 150 years, depending if we understand the water level of the body and the composition of the materials that we put into the body. So, good diet and hydration are essential for long life.

Asthma, allergies, arthritis, hypertension, depression, headaches, diabetes, obesity, and multiple sclerosis are some of the conditions and diseases that are caused by persistent dehydration.

Dr. Batmanghelidij teaches the fundamentals of salt being vital because it extracts and gets rid of acids. So, salt is vital for balancing the acidity of the cell. That's how the body becomes alkaline, because salt extracts the hydrogen ion and then the ion is taken to the kidneys and is flushed out if there is enough water. If there is not enough water, the body cannot detox and flush toxins like it was designed to.

The only way we can become happy by our own design is learning how to become healthy by our own hand. Healthy choices pave the way to a healthy, happy life.

Nutrients
Grounding energizes our food
Photosynthesis Process
- ALKALINITY -

Picture this: our bodies are more alkaline so we want to eat alkaline foods to keep our healthy pH balance which means we need to eat fruits and vegetables and basically anything that is grown from the ground and is part of the earth, just like we are. Okay, next these fruits and vegetables go through the photosynthesis process, they get the nutrients from the soil, the water to hydrate, the air and the sunlight to grow and this action is precisely what make us grow and feeds us in the same way. Not to mention, have you ever noticed how houseplants don't do nearly as well as the plants outside? Indoor plants aren't getting the atmospheric energy from ground, the sunlight and the worldly elements outside to nourish them and to keep them at 100% healthy.

Movement

Movement is also essential to our health. I like the activity and non-activity that is restorative yoga, with its all supported resting poses.

Yoga - Activity

What I know to be true is through exercise we not only reinforce our capabilities to move but we also flush oxygen into our brain and blood to keep our function at a level 10 when we regularly increase our heartbeat through movement. We also hit on the effects of our lymphatic system through jumping, running, and aerobic movement and why we get healthier when we exercise is that it helps detoxify our systems. When our systems are toxic, we want more toxicity. But when we consume vitamins, we become energized and hunger for more.

Yoga can help relieve daily aches and pains, improve the immune system, build muscle strength, increase flexibility, perfect your posture, prevent cartilage and joint breakdown, protect your spine, improve bone health, increase blood flow (circulation), drain your lymph system and boost your immunity, increase your heart rate, drop your blood pressure, regulate your adrenal glands, and help you lose weight and eat less. Yoga lowers your blood sugar levels, helps you focus, releases tension, helps you sleep, gives your lungs room to breathe, prevents IBS and other digestive problems, gives you peace in your mind, increases your self-esteem, and improves mental health. I hope those are enough reasons to get you into a yoga practice. Even if an individual has a health condition like diabetes or heart disease, yoga can significantly alleviate some of the symptoms. It's a win-win.

But if yoga seems too strenuous for you, there is another option.

Non-Activity Restorative Yoga

The first time I tried restorative yoga, I was in Las Vegas visiting a friend and I wanted to keep up on my yoga practice. He owned a health café within a certain gym called Bodi Café and was able to get me in for free so I checked the yoga calendar and found a class, and I was ready to roll. I arrived and to my surprise the class participants were lying down with blankets and blocks and things to which I was not accustomed. The teacher encouraged me to stay; however, I didn't want to because I wanted a "real" workout. She said, "You can thank me later," and then she winked. She had help set me up for my "resting poses" and we went through the one-hour class by spending five to seven minutes resting into each pose. It was a relief, oddly enough; it put me into a state of such peace that my brain started operating like a mastermind. I left that class with three business plans. It's a wonder what being restful will do to us. Per the instructor, people lose more weight doing Restorative Yoga than they do other types of yoga because it relieves the body of being in a "fight or flight" mode and stops the production of cortisol, leaving us in a relaxed, stress-free state.

I highly recommend you try this time of yoga.

MEDITATION

"Meditation triggers the hypothalamus; stimulating the pituitary gland to release endorphins, promoting relaxation, self-healing and overall wellbeing," according to the editors of the Harvard Health Publications division of Harvard Medical School.

For years I have struggled with not believing in myself. People always say, "Just go with your gut" or listen to what your intuition is telling you. I have always relied on my friends to help me make final decisions for the choices I should be making for myself. The truth is, I have felt lost my whole life…or at least until the day I closed my eyes.

In my quest to be self-sufficient, I picked up the most powerful practice we have available to us today: meditation. Meditation has allowed me to clear the pollution from so many years filling my brain with garbage. I can now hear my inner self and I am one with the cells in my body. If I had to pick one thing I could not live without, it would be my ability to connect with my subconscious. Our sixth sense is here the whole time just waiting for us to dust it off and begin to live the way we were meant to. It is our bodies' natural abilities to live happily. We were created to be able to withstand and adapt to most any environment. We can train for marathons, have babies, be contortionists and break world records to do most anything by training ourselves to. Meditation has helped get people who practice it to reach grand success levels, such as Steve Jobs, Oprah Winfrey, Hugh Jackman, Paul McCartney, to name a few. See what a few famous people have to say about it:

"Meditation is helping you to tap into something that's already inside of you... that's you, in essence. That's something that was super-empowering for me once I grasped that." — **Cameron Diaz**

"In meditation, I can let go of everything. I'm not Hugh Jackman. I'm not a dad. I'm not a husband. I'm just dipping into that powerful source that creates everything. I take a little bath in it. Nothing has ever opened my eyes like Transcendental Meditation has. It makes me calm and happy, and, well, it gives me some peace and quiet in what's a pretty chaotic life!" — **Hugh Jackman**

"I start the day with Transcendental Meditation. It puts me in the best mood!" — **Katy Perry**

"In moments of madness, meditation has helped me find moments of serenity." — **Sir Paul McCartney**

"One of the things – and this comes from someone who was highly self-critical and a type-A personality – that has changed my life is meditating." — **Sheryl Crow**

The process is simple: our thoughts come and our brain processes them. Instead of walking around consciously worrying about aspects of your life, let meditation work the bugs out for you. I wished I would have made time for it sooner, but everyone has his or her own process and timing for the things. I would highly suggest hiring a transcendental meditation coach and you can find one near you by going to their website at www.tm.org. I did, and the universe now serves me. What my subconscious wants it gets.

To be able to break free from your life and surroundings is a gift. There is a gift in everything we just need to be aware of what that is. They say our eyes are the gateway to our soul, I couldn't find that to be any closer to the truth.

Meditation has been proven to reduce inflammation and gives us a superpower ability to recover quickly from stressful situations. Just by closing our eyes and taking a break, we can process quickly and efficiently. It also helps IBS and digestive relief, the easing of cold symptoms, and regulating blood pressure. Meditation has even been shown to beat morphine in reducing pain.

It can even help you look younger.

The last part of my life-changing tool kit is for you to break habits by keeping your eye on the "prize."

Habit Changing Tools

I've struggled with smoking cigarettes since I had my first at 12 years old. Growing up, I spent time raising my younger brothers and a ton of time with baby sitters. When mom was working, we were getting into trouble. Bad decisions started at a young age for me. Because I was the oldest child, I took a lot of influence from babysitters and people who were older than me. Looking back, I realize that I grew up too fast, and this is probably an understatement. I watched what the adults were doing, and as any child does, I was curious and experimental.

Long story short I was smoking in no time. With my girlfriends it was a way for us to be adults and be sneaky and live our own lives. We would sneak cigarettes from our parents and older siblings and some even bought them for us at the local gas station. Back in the early '90s some of the gas stations would even sell the cigarettes to us. We would ride our bikes and go hide behind the backstops at the schools, and also on the weekends, we thought were cool when we smoked cigarettes. Though it was gross at the time, I guess it was something for us to do on our own time with our own lives. Besides that, the older kids were doing it and it was the thing to do. But eventually I became hooked.

Years later at the age of 38, one of my best friends, who was a bartender of all people, asked if I'd like to get rid of alcohol for Lent. I thought this was a fantastic idea, and since Lent is 40 days, it was the perfect opportunity for me to get a head start on not smoking. My thoughts were if I could make it 40 days without drinking, I could make it 40 days without smoking because for me they go hand-in-hand. I had known from experience back in my early twenties about substituting one for the other tool set. If I was going to get rid of alcohol and cigarettes, I had best set myself up for success and add two things that were healthy in their places. Doing so would launch some great habits and give me some power moving forward. I decided to do yoga and drink plenty of water instead of drinking alcohol and smoking.

I did extremely well during this 40-day period. I spent a lot of time at home because I didn't want to be triggered out at the bar, which was my usual waste of time. I did yoga, started reading books here and there, and was consciously trying to be really good to myself and treat my body with respect. It was a different life and it took some getting used to. I'd say the first 30 days were unbearable. I had to beat back the urges, sit on my hands and try to control myself for the sake of my future and for the sake of my existence…until something miraculous happened, about six weeks later. I was cruising down the street headed to work. I had Christmas Carols playing on the stereo even though it was in June. My windows were rolled down. I was blasting Christmas Carols and singing along when I noticed something, something was different but very noticeable in my mind, and it was the unmistakable feeling that I was happy. Not only happy, but uncontrollably happy. I was aware of myself in the moment, of being happy, with a legitimate smile and substance behind that smile. I was walking on sunshine; surely, you've had that feeling before. I had always heard of the phrase "being in the moment", but I was never able to experience this because my "moments" raced so quickly and quite frankly, I was afraid of the moment. My moments were filled with fear and anxiety about what I was doing and where I was going in my life, always hanging on me like a backpack of bricks. But at this moment, I loved my life. I loved the air, I loved the day, I loved my car and I loved the way I felt so I pulled over to the side of the road. I flipped down the visor and looked at myself in the mirror and thought, so this is what happy looks like. I was in love with this new moment; this state of mine was my mental note that my direction was good. My choices and hard work had placed me on the right path. I was finally at peace. I was not upset about what I had done the day before, I wasn't mad at the day in front of me and for the very first time, I wasn't worried about tomorrow. No, I felt really happy and excited, which I hadn't felt in years, probably since I was a kid. It was a wholesome type of normalcy that I was free as a bird. I knew that this was definitely due to the no alcohol, cigarettes, and no marijuana smoke fogging my moments. I looked at the calendar and calculated exactly how much time it had gone by and it was six weeks on the dot. I said to myself, six weeks! So that's how long it takes to get your happy back. I like it and I'm honored to share my story with you.

A few days later, when the 40-day period of lent was over my girlfriend and I went to a Warriors' game and ended up having a glass of wine. The wine gave me anxiety, which was a great reminder of why I thought quitting was a fantastic idea to begin with. So, I had another until I was having fun with the group. We all decided since we were drinking, we would Uber back to the house where we would stay the night since we were all too intoxicated to drive. There I was, not being in control of my own life again and on someone else's couch instead of my own bed. I went to sleep and woke up the next day to drive home and go to work, as it was a Saturday that day. A Saturday in the world of hairdressing is the busiest. It wasn't cool when I woke up feeling like a trains wreck with a full schedule ahead. I walked around the house and gathered my belongings taking mental note of my "moment," and a question popped into my head, I wonder how long it's going to take me to get my happy feeling back? Feeling like I was just hit by a bus would make it that much more difficult to help my clients look their best. But I made my bed and I was going to be a big girl and lay in it. If you could actually imagine being sick to your stomach and having the responsibility of doing hair for the next eight hours and not losing your clients in the meantime, being a hairdresser is not so fun anymore. So there I went again, taking the natural fun right out of my life and ruining it with my poor decision.

Six days later, I was at my boyfriend's the morning after a house party, where I had some champagne and yep, you guessed it, cigarettes. I was growing tired of making bad decisions for myself and becoming closer to what's really right for me in my life. My boyfriend was in the shower and I was watching television while evaluating my life, when I had a moment of clarity. In front of me on the television screen is the commercial that would change my life forever. 1- 800-no-butts was giving away free counseling sessions for those who wanted to quit smoking. I thoughts to myself, yeah, there's a lot of things I wanted to quit for good and cigarettes was one of them. What better way to do it than with a professional, so I made the phone call. That phone call would change my life forever. I definitely knew my way around counseling and how much it can benefit a person, with making positive changes in their lives. It piqued my interest in the way that I could not wait to jump on the phone and see what was in store. I was on the phone with the dear woman who was taking me through a series of questions to qualify me and make sure I was truly serious about quitting. They were serious and for good reason as they didn't want to waste their time on anyone who wasn't really ready. Her name was Teresa. She asked me how long I had gone without smoking and I told her it was about five days. She replied, really? That's great. What made you go back to it? I told her that I had a really long Saturday at work and I felt like a cigarette would be the only way I could really relax and unwind from my busy week and day. Teresa thought this was an interesting key factor and she had to know what it was that I did for a living. When I told Teresa that I was an industry hairstylist she quickly replied, "Oh that makes complete sense." I want you to get a piece of paper and a pen so you can write this word down: COMPASSION FATIGUE.

I thought, I've heard this word before, and I was curious to know where she was going with it. Teresa explained to me that most in the service industry on some level have compassion fatigue from empathetically listening to other people's problems. The professionals that are mostly affected from this type of fatigue are firefighters, police officers, judges, counselors and therapist of all sorts, lawyers, and hairdressers. All are susceptible to uploading the compassion from their clients. There are exercises that you can do to correct this on a daily basis so you feel better without having to run towards self-medication of any form. Just have a look online and you'll find all kinds of ways. She then proceeded to tell me to turn the piece of paper over and in the middle of the piece of paper she wanted me to write a big T in the middle of it. On the left- hand side of the top of the T she wanted me to write the word "triggers" and on the right side she wanted me to write the word "prize."

At this point my boyfriend was out of the shower and he was standing over me interested in what was going on the phone that I could be possibly taking notes. Teresa counseled me on what my triggers were that made me want to smoke. I wrote things like alcohol, other stimulating drugs, celebrations, socializing of any sort, driving, taking a break at work and any stressful situation, good times and the bad. Then we went over to the prize category; Teresa had me write something very interesting on the top of that category – my cravings would only last for three to five minutes. This was most valuable information because I knew what to expect, which is half the battle. For me, learning about the why something is happening and the process of what will happen helps me get through to the other end because knowledge is power.

Below the cravings I felt inspired to write, "keep your eye on the prize!"

Under the prize category we explored why I was making this change and how it was important to my life. What I would get from being successfully smoke-free? In this category I wrote things like to be healthy, be happy, smell good, be physically fit, not be frowned upon. I wanted to fit in with the people who love themselves because

I was not one of those people. I wanted to become one of those people.

Above all of this I would live a long, healthy life free of getting any types of cancers, and I would be able to attract a man who also took his life seriously. We would go on caring for ourselves happily ever after. This was something I wanted a great deal.

In another category we listed things I could do instead of smoking cigarettes. In particular, I wrote clean my car, clean my clothes and clean my teeth so I could start fresh and be fresh! I would surround myself with those that were making healthy choices in life, which was an intelligent thing to do. I wanted to be more intelligent so I would surround myself such. I talked about having my teeth cleaned and having the beautiful white healthy smile to be proud of. Having fresh breath being in the service industry is key, and for dating, having fresh breath is inviting. I would also be health conscious of the food I would eat so I could live an even healthier life. This all sounded like it would turn me into the person I was meant to be. But first I had a lot of work to do and it wasn't going to be easy.

My next steps were to quit smoking the very next day. I already had a pack of Chantix (a smoking cessation drug) that I was going to use for the first week or two so I could get some time under my belt. Chantix helps block the nicotine receptors in your brain so the urge goes away. It worked wonders for me.

The drug makers urged caution and suggested you take it under the care of a physician because the side effects have been known to make people depressed, if you have had prior history of depression. Lucky for me, I've always been a very happy person, and the drug made me a little happier. I am sure my happiness came from not having the anxiousness for my next cigarette. What was most important was that it served a purpose of getting me through the tough part of being without a cigarette.

The process wasn't easy, but I made it one-week, and then to the 30-day mark, and the three-month mark, and the one-year mark. A big thank you to my coach Teresa at 1800-no-butts, my tool kit, and keeping my eye my prize! My why was so important to me that it kept me pushing along.

To this day, almost three years later, I am still smoke-free, alcohol-free, drug-free, and I have added so many beautiful things and wonderful experiences into my life, which continues to grow each day.

My why is what keeps me going and yours can, too.

I am very excited to see and hear how my story, and the tools and my success have inspired you live a happier life. My hope is that you will share yours with not only me, but with the world around you as well. We all need to be inspired; it's what keeps us going!

Please share with me by adding your 800-nobutts tool kit worksheet through my website happybydesignbook.com or e-mail me at emily@emilywyant.com so I can share in the celebration!

I can't wait to see how you are making all of your dreams come true.

Made in the USA
Monee, IL
02 February 2021